KICKING UP TROUBLE

UPLAND BIRD HUNTING
IN THE WEST

John Holt

Kicking Up Trouble
Upland Bird Hunting in the West

John Holt

Illustrated By

Christopher S. Smith

Wilderness Adventures Press™
Bozeman, Montana

Published by Wilderness Adventures Press™
P.O. Box 1410
Bozeman, MT 59771

10 9 8 7 6 5 4 3 2 1

Printed in the United States of America

Library of Congress Catalog Card Number:

ISBN 1-885106-02-5
Limited Edition of 250   ISBN 1-885106-03-3

In memory of my good friends Omar and Uncle Scotty

Table of Contents

Introduction

Welcome to Holt's World

The first time I met John Holt was at the witching hour — what writer James Crumley calls "dark-thirty" — during one of those wicked vernal blizzards with which Montana likes to welcome the unsuspecting sportsman. I was at Chico Hot Springs with Silvio Calabi, the editor of *Fly Rod & Reel*, fishing the spring creeks in Paradise Valley. We were staying in a cabin on the grounds. After a late supper, Calabi had muttered something about a guy named Holt who might join us the next day, then toddled off to bed.

I stayed up past midnight, reading and unwinding from the day's action. Outside the sleet beat down, the wind wailed, sheets of whiteout hissed passed the window. My kind of night. Then through the noise of the storm, I heard a vehicle approaching — a wheezing, catarrhal sound, like the death rattle of a World War I mustard gas victim. The truck chugged to a halt near the cabin. I heard the tinny slam of its door, booted footsteps on the wooden stairs.

A heavy fist pounded.

What the hell could this be? Only a masochist, a madman, or a serial killer would be out on a night like this.

When I opened the cabin door, my suspicions seemed confirmed. Before me stood a tall, gaunt, red-eyed man with a three days' growth of beard. The well-chewed stub of a black cigar smoldered like a burning landfill in the corner of his mouth. Big-knuckled hands caked in dried blood protruded from the sleeves of his muddy jacket; baggy-kneed Levis hung from his hips. Then in the bed of the truck, half hidden by a sleet-caked tarp, I saw the source of the blood — the corpses of two sharp-spurred, long-bearded Merriam's turkeys.

I was instantly reassured. After all, your stone bird-hunter is capable of any excess.

"I'm Holt," the apparition said with a shy, sly grin, "and I've been driving through this crap like...well...forever. You got a drink?"

I did indeed, and poured him one.
It was the start of a beautiful friendship.

John Holt has made his name over the past few years as the nation's most outspoken angling writer. He can write tough, he can write funny, he can write real, and he's not afraid to express his opinions — even when they call down upon him the death threats of clear-cutting loggers or the nattering pique of politically correct flyfishing mavens. That he can also write about upland bird hunting — with a clear eye and a sense of country, vistas, weather, heat, cold, pain, thirst, joy, and footsore delight in a way not seen since the heyday of Bob Ruark or Gordon MacQuarrie — should make us all rejoice. But it shouldn't surprise us.

"Flyfishing is part of my bird hunting and vice versa," he writes in this book. "It's all hunting when you come down to it."

And it is if you do it right. When we're fishing, we often discover good bird covers, and when we're hunting we sometimes stumble across new, promising streams that we'll return to in due season. But it's more than that: Each time we go out with a rod or gun in our hands, we're hunting something inchoate and elusive within ourselves. I call it The Wild Weasel, and you can rest assure that John Holt's found his, wherever he roams.

An unfortunate distinction between "angler" and "hunter" has been with us since the days of the sainted Isaak Walton (witness Piscator and Venator in *The Compleat Angler*), and it's grown even sharper today, with the concept of "catch-and-release" making anglers the good guys and the burgeoning societal fear of guns turning hunters — even bird hunters — into stereotyped blackhats. Whatever happened to the umbrella term "Sportsman" which, in my youth, used to encompass all of us who both hunted and fished, whenever we got the chance, and never saw the difference? It's been co-opted these days by guys who play the ponies, chase skirts, or spend every weekday swilling beer in front of the big-screen TV watching the great big wild card quarterfinals of the SuperBowlWorldSeriesStanleyCupNBAPlayoffs.

John Holt is a Sportsman in the old sense of the word, and he says to hell with that stuff.

When the world gets too much with him (about once every couple of days, it seems), he throws some flyrods, guns, and cheap cigars into his Toyota "beater," along with a greasy tarp, a funky sleeping bag, a cooler full of wine, beer, bourbon, and nutritious foodstuffs — emphasis in the latter category falling on well-marbled steaks or pork chops, high-smelling cheeses, fresh greens, Paul Newman's Salad Dressing, crusty breads, and delicate desserts like Twinkies. Then he splits for the High Lonesome.

I've been in enough of Holt's makeshift camps by now to have learned to love them. Usually they're in stark, strong, arid country — less chance of meeting other people when you have to drag your own water — where the only company is coyotes, bears, eagles, and snarling buffalo gnats. There's a quickly assembled fire ring of whatever rocks happen to be lying around, a pile of deadfall lodgepole or ponderosa for fuel, maybe a hunk of alligator tailmeat blackening over the flames, crisp-skinned Idaho bakers steaming in the coals, and nearby a bottle of Jack Daniels leaning atilt — the Wreck of the Mary Deare, winking redly in the firelight.

If there's a river nearby, John will fish it well into darkness — he never whoops or exults when he hooks a big trout, but if you're fishing nearby you can hear the powerful splash of the take and feel Holt's vibes hit the redline. If it's snowing or raining, he'll fish longer, sometimes all night. If you're hunting, you'll often find yourself at dusk about ten miles from camp, legs turned to Silly Putty, mouth so dry you're spitting cotton, the gun now having increased its weight to twenty-five pounds, and John urging you up just one more ridge for those elusive goddam chukars. Or whatever....

"Hey, man, if they fly against this moonrise, *they'll be backlit!*"

There's no mealtime or bedtime in one of John's camps. You get back when you get there, as he says, and pour yourself a drink, grab a tin plate of whatever's cooking, kick back by the fire on your sleeping bag, and have at it. For a short while it sounds like a pack of lobo wolves that's just dragged down a baldface steer: slurping, chomping, belching, and growling, punctuated now and then by the dulcet sound of soldier beans, if they're on the menu, and sometimes when they're not. If there's a dog along, all the better — no leftovers to scrape into the fire. Later, there's cleaning the birds and guns, the firelight stiff on your windburned face, maybe getting up occasionally to walk off a cramp in your knotted legs. That's when the talk starts.

"The best of all talk," Faulkner called it in *The Bear*. "It was of the wilderness, the big woods, bigger and older than any record-ed document — of white man fatuous enough to believe he had bought any fragment of it, or Indian ruthless enough to pretend that any fragment of it was his to convey...".

Our talk always begins with the birds or the fish of that day, how they behaved, where they were using, what they took or how they flew; then of other birds or fish of the past that acted the same, or perhaps differently; of other creatures encountered along the way (spiders, snakes, grizzlies); of shots or hookups missed (never of what we killed or landed); of wind, and of light on rock or water; odd sounds, strange manifestations — dust devils and dis-tant, soundless lightning, perhaps, or a flint-knapped arrowhead found in the middle of nowhere, or maybe a strange old hunk of stone — the petrified pizzle of a Giant Plains-Roving Dire Elk?

The talk swings to books and writing, then veers off (say) into little-known lore of the Plains Indians, imaginings of what it must have been like to ride down buffalo bareback at full gallop and kill them with short, powerful bows backed by the pliant horn of wild sheep and obsidian-tipped arrows — or to shoot sharptails in the early days with muzzle-loading shotguns, when there were birds everywhere (and Indians, too) — or of the days of the beaver men and how tough they must have been — Glass and Smith and Bridger and old Broken Hand Fitzpatrick, Zenas Leonard and Osborne Russell, Liver-Eating Johnson, Jim Clyman who survived more than a decade of trapping the Rockies back in the 1820s only to return East and get bushwhacked and nearly scalped by a couple of scruffy Winnebago bucks near Wauwatosa, Wisconsin, where I used to live and Clyman once had a sawmill. Holt starts telling stories about his own youth in the Badger State, of covering the police beat in Beloit, or fishing muskies in the fall up north — we have all that in common, the hunting and fishing, newspapers, and Wisconsin boyhoods. The love of wild country.

And a whole lot more.

Then suddenly, in a moment of silence with the meniscus of the whiskey bottle ebbed to low tide for the evening, it occurs to me that the talk around the campfires of the mountain men nearly two centuries ago must have been much like our talk this evening. Perhaps even similar, thematically at least, to the talk of the earliest hunters sitting around their own feeble flames at the dawn of time, picking strands of mammoth meat from between their teeth.

As if to underscore that fancy, a coyote begins to sing on a distant ridge, and all across the wilderness — eons away — others join the chorus.

This book reads like one of the best of those evenings.

"Killing birds is only a part of it," John says toward the end of the volume. Amen to that. Make no mistake, though: Plenty of birds die in these pages — Huns and chukars, ringnecks and sharptails, turkeys and sage grouse and mountain grouse (you'll just love the fool hen chapter) — and still others fly off unscathed, as they do in real life. But John Holt's true alchemy is to have made this far more than "just another hunting book."

It's no less than a heartsong to the Wild Weasel in all of us.

Welcome to Holt Country!

Robert F. Jones

Acknowledgements

I would like to acknowledge the unflagging support and friendship from the publishers of this book, Chuck and Blanche Johnson, owners of Wilderness Adventures — two people who make the writing game worthwhile. Also, editor Steve Smith turned this into a much better bit of work and became a good friend in the process. Others who have come to the rescue with advice and information include Tony Acerrano, Steve Bodio, Jake How, Tim Joern, Bob Jones, Tim Linehan, and Michael McIntosh. Lastly, thanks for the patience exhibited by the people I live for — Lynda, of course, and Jack, Elizabeth, and Rachel.

Prologue

When we saw an eagle turn over the empty road we stopped in a kind of ecstasy and got out to stand on the roadside to breathe and turn in circles and wave our arms. What was this place?

Stephen Bodio, *Querencia*

What was this place? The question I've always asked whenever I'm out standing in the middle of the high plains of Montana, gun in hand, a tough sun and cutting wind burning my face. Isolated pockets of mountains dot the immensity like lonely ships becalmed on an ancient, unknown sea under a cloudless sky. The snow and ice-covered Rocky Mountain Front tears straight up for thousands of feet above the flat stretches of native grasses and sere grain fields. The air is cool, even now in mid-September, as it moves with purpose down from the rough peaks out over this apparent emptiness.

How did I get here and where is "here"? After decades of wandering the West, the land is as familiar to me as an old friend, but like the best of them, never the same from one day to the next. There's a sense of familiarity not quite recognized in this country. I know I've been here before, but I'm not sure when. "Was it yesterday?" and my companions often laugh when they see the familiar expression of puzzlement.

"Should have gone to bed earlier last night, Holt," they'll say.

And they're probably right, but I've noticed similar looks on their faces at times. The situation is more than late-night conversations and whiskey and too little sleep. The peaks and prairies of the West are powerful stuff. Occasional disorientation is part of their game.

My friend and I watch as his German wirehair works with energy I can only dream of, back and forth, nose down as he tracks sharptails hiding in the volunteer wheat that has yet to be knocked down by rough weather or relentless machinery. We're all alone up here on this dry bench that gives way to coulees and then still more table-topped bluffs. This is the way the land was 500 years ago, the way I hope it will always remain — wild, untouched, just on the edge of being frightening and lonely.

We walk in behind the dog now on point and five, eight, a dozen sharps blast out of gray and brown grass. The growth is thick, matted like an old throw rug. How do the grouse fly out of here so quickly? Their wings pound against the air as they fight to gain purchase, to zip fast downwind away from trouble. Each of us fires, both barrels, and two birds drop, rolling into the earth, small clouds of feathers riding the breeze like natural exhaust. One grouse for each of us. Already more than enough on this early autumn day, but there would be more birds and shooting. The dog would see to that.

Upland bird hunting in the West, and Montana in particular, is far different from the shooting of the north woods of Wisconsin or the thick covers of Vermont. Sure, there is plenty of tight work for mountain grouse such as the ruffed, but hunting out here is also characterized by miles of openness that never seems to end. Your eyes cannot see far enough. From the first Saturday in September through the end of November, I wander these prairies in search of sage and sharp-tailed grouse, chukar, Hungarian partridge, turkey, and pheasant. Back home in the northwest corner, west of the Continental Divide, there are ruffed, blue, and spruce grouse to hunt; cold, breezy ridges to walk in search of the blues or thick stands of larch and fir to slip through seeking the other two.

All fine country wherever I look. I can never get enough of it. Sandhill cranes and doves are also considered upland birds out here, but they involve different techniques and engender different types of shooting in my eyes. Great birds hanging out in excellent land, but they belong in another book written by someone else.

This book is about hunting the grouse and partridge and pheasants during the course of one season, only three months, a period of time that begins in the heat of late summer and stretches relentlessly toward winter. There are days when the hunting approaches tedium, seems too damn long, but then in the first days of December when the shooting is over, I wonder if fall was ever here at all. Like the years as I get older, the weeks afield vanish too quickly. The edge-softening qualities of memory will have to do the heavy work of carrying me through the long months until another golden September.

All of this is ancient history that hasn't happened yet on this bright day. My friend and his dog are side-hilling it along the edge of a draw thick with chokecherry and strips of tangled alder growing in some moist cuts. Tough going, even for the dog. Suddenly, that familiar sound of wings reaches me, riding on the warm wind, for the sun still packs some heat in the afternoon.

A lone sharptail powers up quickly, skimming the ground as it crests the bluff. Everything is in slow motion — mountains flashing all around me; the dark blue of the sky cutting hard against the muted colors of the land; the orange of my friend's hat; and the dog half in the air, pointing in still life at the bird as it flies toward me not seventy yards away.

I take my time bringing the gun up and pushing off the safety, swinging smoothly through the bird as it soars by. The Beretta goes off as I look at the target, not seeing the barrels, not conscious of pulling the trigger. Then this grouse whirls in mid-air with a puff of feathers before hitting the ground in a soft *whomp*.

Everything happened in seconds, but lasted again forever. The world comes back to life, its velocity now in synch with the rest of things, but that one shot defined bird hunting not just for the day or a year, but for all seasons. That is why I'm out here.

John Holt
Whitefish, Montana

Chapter One

Sage Grouse

As with anything in life, reality is a matter of perception. Flyfishing for large, aggressive brown trout in a November snowstorm may be fun for me, perhaps necessary. I know for a fact it is hell on earth for others. Within hours they are cold, surly, and in dire need of strong drink and a warm fire.

This is also true of hunting sage grouse in the eastern half of Montana, and, for that matter, many other spots around the West. To many, the miles of sagebrush prairie that roll off in all directions beneath several lesser mountain ranges are barren wasteland. This is country many of us avoid as we sail by, bound for more productive cover.

Even the most casual excursions out into the heart of this terrain on a hot, early autumn afternoon will tend to confirm this negative assessment. Well-worn boots kick up puffs of alkali dust; the air quietly sizzles in the white heat that blasts back up from the ground into your face; there is no breeze, not a trace of a zephyr to be felt. Water is a fond memory growing dimmer in the clear light. Cotton mouth and an overpowering thirst dominate the few remaining coherent thoughts that rattle through a sizzling brain pan. If you're lucky, you will be bitten by a few mosquitoes hanging around the scraggly, iron-stemmed clumps of gray-green sagebrush. If fortune turns its capricious back on you, some form of nasty spider may inflict a painful bite on a leg or under your sweat-stained shirt. Obviously, this is good country. There can be no argument on this point.

The groups of antelope that are often a common sight in this land have vanished, long gone, searching for more benign

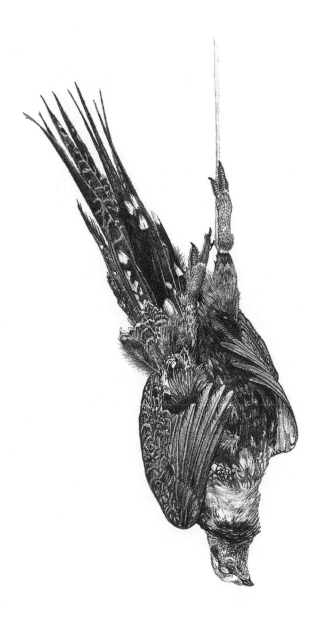

country — perhaps a little water and a touch of shade, not this parched madness. The deer aren't around either. They're huddled up in the cool of the forested slopes on the distant mountains, or they're hiding in the sweet dampness of a brushy creekbed.

The landscape looks abandoned, like an old ghost town whose ramshackle saloons and gaudy storefronts are crumbling inexorably into the dirt, a dead zone cooking silently alone — the high plains of real life. Not the glorified, wild boom towns, gunfights, and fast horses of the movies or commercial-ridden TV shows. The honest article.

Far better to concentrate one's efforts looking for pheasants in the stream bottoms, or along narrow intermittent springs clogged with emerald green patches of watercress, or drainage ditches that wind through the solid waves of hills, bluffs, and arroyos that dominate this vastness. Even the fields of wheat turning dry and light brown in the furnace atmosphere look more promising.

Initial, cursory examinations and hastily formed opinions are frequently deceptive, inaccurate. Looking closer, spending more time, changes first impressions. This is true for this part of Montana. In addition to several kinds of rodents tunneling away with mindless abandon just beneath the parched surface — and along with countless noisome species of biting insects, rattlesnakes of varying lengths and thicknesses, and arachnids that are crawling all over the place — there is a creature that finds this seeming banquet of hostility a safe, secure home.

Settled in among this down-scale forest of scrub growth is a bird of surprising size and abundance. The sage grouse, resembling more a small turkey than a grouse, thrives under these trying conditions. Males will often reach thirty inches in length and occasionally exceed seven pounds. Sometimes called sage hens, the bird have re-established themselves in the West. They are now found from east of the Rockies in Montana to Wyoming. They're present in huntable numbers in northern Colorado, pockets of the western Dakotas, and in southern Alberta. West of the Continental Divide, they are found in a very few isolated spots in western Montana as well as in southern Idaho, eastern Oregon, northern Utah, northeast California, and eastern Washington.

The species is now back in sufficient numbers to provide unique shooting, after rushing toward the awful permanence of oblivion. Extensive habitat destruction wrought by mammoth agrarian, sod-busting operations forced them to wage a precarious balancing act on the frightening edge for decades.

Sage grouse are the second-largest gallinaceous (chicken-like) game bird on the continent; only wild turkeys run larger. The cocks average a little less than six pounds, and the hens run slightly larger than a rooster pheasant.

Admittedly sharptails, Huns, and pheasants attract the ardent attentions of many more of us who carry shotguns than does the oft-maligned sage grouse, but that is the hunter's loss and does not reflect unkindly on the genetic composition of the birds themselves, which are highly adapted to one of the harshest environments in North America.

While the sage grouse presents a large target, watching a six-pound bird rise into the air in a lumbering motion of alternately beating wings and then swift glides is a study in apparent contradiction. How can any bird so big and ungainly in appearance attain speed so quickly? The wings are longer than those of other grouse, and this aids in flight. Quick reactions on the part of the hunter result in relatively easy shots as the birds attempt to escape far downrange. No bee-buzzing Hungarian antics for this bird. If for some reason, and in my case there are frequently many, you do not get on your bird immediately, he will roar out of effective pattern range with surprising efficiency. A healthy target turns small in a hurry.

On a September hunt in central Montana during the height of a bluebird afternoon, my companion's vizsla kicked up a sage grouse that took flight and was instantly dropped. While we admired the bird and I took some photographs of the event, another grouse took off from the same location the first leaped from, which was where I happened to be standing. I released the camera and frantically raised my gun only to realize that the grouse was halfway to the small but delightful community of Big Timber in the south. The shot I finally took did kill the bird, which soared mortally injured to another clump of sage a quarter-mile downwind. Fortunately, the dog hunted up the downed grouse.

What this incident demonstrates is how quickly the species is able to reach escape velocity. Switching from camera to gun took mere seconds, but already the bird was almost home free, well out of any effective pattern, the shot string about to plop harmlessly on the dusty ground well behind.

I've wondered why the sage grouse evolved into an animal capable of rapid flight that is all but unnecessary for eluding ground-based predators and yet insufficient to escape the lethal attentions of prey circling the skies above. What's the point? Additionally, no other game bird is so dependent on so few food sources as this grouse. While this is certainly not anomalous behavior or specious adaptation in a climate where a foot of rainfall in a twelve-month period takes on monsoon-like, if not heroic, proportions, it is species-specific and of some tactical interest to the shooter.

In colder months, the bird's diet is almost exclusively sage. It doesn't have a grinding gizzard like other grouse, so it is able to ingest only relatively soft plant material like the leaves of the sage plant. Water comes from dew and plant material most of the time. This varies only slightly in spring and summer when the grouse dine graciously on insects like grasshoppers and also feed in nearby fields of alfalfa and wheat. In other words, as the hunting season advances and the average temperature declines, the combination of sagebrush and water translates into finding grouse. A simple, elegant equation.

At first sight, sagebrush looks like a plant that you can just walk through or over. Nothing could be farther from reality. The base of the plant is as unyielding and tough as tempered steel. Smaller limbs are as wiry and tough as old boot leather. Branches spring back with swift vengeance, leaving welts and bruises that take days to heal. Thick congregations of the plant translate into tough days in the field. At night, after eight hours or so of trudging through the sage flats, your legs feel like they are still pushing through fence wire or stepping on coiled springs, your shins afire from the hammering of the plant's limbs.

In this tough, arid jungle classified as northern desert, the sage grouse finds the necessities of life, which are not all that different from those required by the rest of us staggering around on the planet: food, shelter-security, and water. A sagebrush prairie is in reality a miniature forest. It is all a matter of perspective, and from the grouse's ground-level point of view, a three-foot tall bush takes on redwood dimensions. In such habitat, a sage hen is lost to much of the predatory world. It is all but invisible to the deadly efforts of hawks gliding hungrily above. The ubiquitous, egg-eating ground squirrel creates far greater mayhem in the grouse's world. Badgers and coyotes are not high on the bird's favorite visitors' list either.

The grouse can travel from copse to copse of sage with impunity. Distances are measured in increments of several feet, vastly reducing the risks commonly associated with movement in open country, the prevailing wisdom being — "don't."

The grouse have been found up as high as 10,000 feet, but in Montana, where they are now most abundant, the grouse are more common in the 4,000- to 5,000-foot range. Out away from the scattered bursts of mountains that dot the central Montana skyline, moisture is an uncommon friend, streams, lakes, and ponds infrequent acquaintances. Find an expanse of sagebrush with a stock pond holding water year-round or a tiny creek trickling along a brief cut in the ground, and you'll find sage hen in good numbers. Add a little Conservation Reserve Program (CRP) acreage early in the season, and you have Designer Habitat. There will be birds and the hunting should be straightforward, productive.

In fact, there is now so much prime bird habitat in the central part of Montana as a result of CRP that, during years of normal rainfall, finding the grouse in the early going can be difficult and frustrating. Everywhere you look there is cover for the birds. There have been times when I've walked through the heat and dust of September looking for the birds where they usually are later in the season. There weren't any. They were all eating and loafing in the tall fields of grains and native grasses that thrive under the aegis of CRP. Locating the grouse in hundreds of thousands of acres is daunting.

Finally, toward sunset, normally near water, the birds come lumbering in from the fields providing a primitive form of pass shooting. Set up ahead of time in the right cover, and the shooting is like duck hunting a salt marsh when the birds come circling in. You'll get a few shots before the grouse panic and then get hip to the danger and strike off in a hurry to another source of water.

The grouse rapidly grow in size as they slide in toward the water in the fading light of late day. They loom ever larger. Rising up out of tall grasses and taking aim is an adrenaline rush when you see the birds finally curve their wings against the air to begin their final approach. The shots are quick swings as the sage hens veer swiftly away at steep angles, fleeing the unfamiliar sight presented by the hunter. With a steady touch and a bit of luck, one or more may pancake into the shallow water. It's all over in a heartbeat.

Even with dogs, hunting is often long, hard, and the action sporadic in September and the first part of October. Many eschew the use of dogs for these birds, and this is sometimes a mistake. Coupled with the difficulty of finding the grouse in the first place is the problem of locating them after they are down. Once shot, they plummet and crash into the sage and thick grasses and grains. If only lightly hit, they run like hell for yards and yards. They can be almost impossible to locate without a good dog. Wasting the birds is wrong. The coyotes can find their own food.

Sage grouse are gregarious by nature, and it is amazing how many of them can pop up into the air from a single batch of sage. Their dark coloration, shading to gray with yellowish toning, blends perfectly with their cover. Early in the season, finding one or two grouse is the rule. By mid-October, groups of fifty or more are spotted wandering the flats and fields in search of food in an area that may also have doubled as a lek or breeding ground during the annual spring mating dance.

After driving hundreds of miles to fish a little-known river for even lesser-known but very large brown trout one cold, windy October afternoon, I pulled over below a sage bluff and set up camp. Even with the swiftly moving bands of cirrus clouds, the day was bright. Too early for the trout. That would be a dusk pursuit when the light was lower and the predatory browns would move out from the undercut shelter of the brushy banks. Until then, I'd climb the nearby draw and hunt the sage hens.

Once on top, the force of the wind whipping down from the Big Horn Mountains to the southeast in Wyoming forced me to lean forward at a mild slant. There was fresh snow on the upper flanks of the range and a taste of winter in the air.

After a mile I spotted the distinctive display of a number of cocks bobbing and weaving as they fed. Maybe a hundred of them. A veritable herd of grouse. Others were either holding motionless or strutting stiff-backed with perceived regality. Tough guys out on the prowl. They looked like roosters with breasts. A curious, wild sight. "Poppings" and dull *thumps* reverberated on across the flat. Evening dinner conversation?

Crouching down, I approached to within thirty yards, maybe less. I worked upwind, so the birds were oblivious to my presence. Sitting concealed behind a large bunch of sage, I watched the birds as they fed steadily on sage, leaves, and perhaps small bugs crawling lethargically on the ground. I was reminded of closing time at a favorite bar in Whitefish. No one really knows what they want, but whatever it is, they want a lot of it. It's Saturday night. Time to pull out all of the stops. Two a.m. and last call was busting through the front door of this high-plains saloon.

After awhile I checked the gun, pushed off the safety, and stood up. Hell was instantly in session. Birds were running, leaping for the air with fast-pounding wings, or just staring in stunned disbelief at my appearance. One crazed human with bulging eyes and thinning hair carrying a weapon. A terrible vision trodding the plains. I swung on a small cock and he fell in a heap. Another broke to my right and he was down too. I could have reloaded and shot another pair, but two seemed more than enough for tonight's dinner over a fire of cottonwood coals. I picked the grouse up, admiring their size and protective coloration. I shoved them in the back of my coat and walked back to camp.

They were excellent fare, basted in olive oil and a little orange juice, seasoned with salt and freshly ground pepper, then grilled over the hot coals. A small pot of wild rice and a bottle of Sauvignon blanc made for an excellent dinner. Eating and drinking like a king in end-of-the-world cactus, spider, snake, and sage country. As I finished off the wine, slight movement tugged at the side of my vision. On a ridge across the river, a small band of antelope, five of them, fed casually. The dark horns and black masks glowed with magenta in the light of the sinking sun. Down closer to the water, a flock of Merriam's turkeys ambled along, heads bobbing up and down, *chirping* and *putting* among themselves about god-knows-what. I think turkeys may be a bit crazy by nature and I can appreciate that.

Wherever I've found upland birds is nice turf, even in empty lots that used to be cornfields but are now awaiting the ruthless attentions of some greedy developer. Sage grouse are more of the same, only the places they hang out in are far from cities and the meddling attentions of people. They need the privacy of wildness as much as I do. Adult supervision, while periodically called for, even desperately needed at times, takes on the trappings of a cerebral straightjacket way out here in the soul of nowhere. If I break a leg, run out of gas, or stay up far too late, so what? I'll take my chances and be a happier boy when I return home.

That's another reason sage grouse are so intriguing. There ain't no Mini-Marts or Super 8 Motels where these birds exist.

Later, near dark, the browns turned out and I caught and released a few on small elk hair caddis dry flies. The fish would take the pattern with a roll that boiled the river's quicksilver surface before lunging and thrashing downstream. By dark I'd had my fill and walked back to camp. After turning the fire back up to a full-scale blaze with some tinder-dry limbs, I smoked a fat Honduran cigar before passing out under a sky jammed with stars and planets. Coyotes barked among themselves in the untamed darkness. I was home again.

Sage grouse are considered an "arena bird," meaning that the males of the species gather in communal courtship in locations that have survived for this purpose for generations. Sharptail, along with greater and lesser prairie chickens, display similar behavior. Often several dozen or more males will engage in competition with each other in order to earn the right to breed with the area's females. About ten percent of the males will eventually mate with approximately seventy-five percent of the hens. Leks of thousands of feet square with several hundred males have been documented.

The males begin their dance early in the spring (around March or April) as soon as the snow has melted on the level, sparsely vegetated areas. Activity begins well before dawn, the early bird syndrome. Individual males stake out roughly a thousand square feet of territory, a piece of property defended with vigor through a series of displays designed to deter other birds. As with most species, the older birds usually hold the prime land — the ground closest to the arena's center where the majority of females will visit for breeding.

Unlike the frantic rushes and dashes of sharps and prairie chickens, sage grouse displays are courtly, bordering on pretentious. Males fan their long, pointed tail feathers and puff up their air sacs as they parade across their personal stage. The birds' heads are scarcely visible amid the piles of fluffy white chest feathers. By steadily gulping large draughts of air, the two yellow-green skin sacs are inflated. Eventually the air is expelled to produce a small "popping" noise. This is followed by a low-pitched purring sound that closely resembles a muffled burp carefully released at a stuffy dinner party following the main course. All the while, breast feathers rub against the wings, sounding like two pieces of canvas brushing together.

When two competing males meet at a territorial border, all manner of raucous behavior, including head pecking, strutting, and bluffing, ensues. Often they'll face each other in a stand-off that dissipates either out of boredom or an unwillingness to extend the hostilities to the next level. Eventually the two combatants will discreetly retreat from the scene and resume their courting displays. Priorities must be observed.

The hens normally nest within several miles of the lek, within easy flying and gliding distance. They lay an average of seven eggs, and by late summer the fledglings are grown, but they still stay near the lek. Migrations occur later in the fall.

Springtime behavior on the lek has all the trappings of high drama, but like most potential bar fights, violence rarely makes an appearance. The idea that hundreds of these large grouse show up out of the emptiness of the plains is minor magic. Country that looks lifeless in the dead of winter comes alive with the first heat of the new year. On a large lek there could literally be over a ton of crazed sage grouse moving in slightly chaotic, synchronous sexual rhythm as they practice their time-honored, high-plains dance.

Despite the fact that sage grouse have re-established themselves in healthy numbers around the West, the days of killing a hundred or more, as many early settlers did, are long gone. Lewis and Clark observed sage hens almost 200 years ago, but by 1906 numbers were already on the wane. In the 1930s, populations were so low that most seasons were closed throughout the West. Improving land management led to seasons opening again in the fifties.

Even in areas that receive hunting pressure, opening day shooting can seem too easy, but within a week the birds' learning curve has risen dramatically. Finding the grouse then can be difficult in the extreme. Once shot at or over, they tend to hold tight or dart between patches of cover (I've spoken with hunters who claimed to have tracked the birds on the ground for a couple of miles) or flush wild. The hunt quickly evolves from your basic target shoot to careful stalking and quick reactions. Hens seem to be more acrobatic, twisting and turning through the air, while the cocks go right about the business of escape with a straight and even-keeled flight path.

In the open, the grouse will not allow a hunter to get close, scattering wildly into draws and other brushy cover, though singles seem to be less wary or alert than coveys. A good dog working these broken singles can provide decent action. Even when a covey flushes, there are often a couple of stragglers that burst up at your feet in a belated attempt at escape.

Aside from using binoculars to sight a lone bird doing a sentry imitation while the rest of the flock holds tight to cover feeding or loafing or nodding off during the middle of the day, one of the easiest and surest ways of locating the grouse is by finding their droppings. Where the birds have roosted, there are piles dumped all over the place. Fresh deposits mean the grouse are around or were recently, though experience indicates they may well be long gone if either predators or hunters have passed by. Older droppings serve only as temporary incentives to keep on trudging with renewed hope. Walking long distances is as much a part of sage grouse hunting, more so than with other species at times, as anything. Tracks around waterholes obviously tell of their presence.

Most hunters are of the inaccurate opinion that sage grouse are poor table fare. Some old males tend to be stringy and so tough that they need to be dragged behind a pickup for a few miles to loosen them up. And the taste of sage can also be a bit much; but a pressure cooker and some judicious seasoning can turn a tough bird into a palatable meal. The smaller the bird, the better the flavor seems to be a mild axiom. Younger birds are good grilled or fried with a bit of olive oil and red wine or even the addition of some dark stout.

Sage grouse are a bird of solitary pursuit for me. I prefer walking them down alone. Once, on the way home from ten days on the road hunting and fishing the plains of Montana, I spotted several birds standing like statues out in the middle of a rolling sage flat. After a couple thousand miles of driving, anything less than eighty miles-per-hour smacked of pedestrian behavior. Noting a wide spot on the edge of the narrow highway, I slammed on the brakes, locking the wheels, the truck breaking loose as the tires slipped over a piece of slick pavement. The world took on all of the aspects of a spinning panorama as I deftly executed a 360-degree turn, coming to rest in a cloud of gravel, pointed the way I'd started, right where I wanted to stop in the first place.

Pushing off a tangled mess of shotgun and flyrod cases, a box of cigars, a small duffel, and a camera case that had worked its way behind my neck, I climbed out of the truck. A travel rod in its black metal case rolled free, clattering its way downhill across the highway and into the grass. A small herd of cattle standing comatose by a gate looked up in mild surprise.

A rancher, before now unseen, working with a spade in a small irrigation ditch, looked up with a wry smile creasing a weathered face. "Hell of a stop. Never quite seen it done that way before."

"It's an acquired trait."

"I noticed that," and we both laughed.

After a little talk over a couple of frosty beers plucked from my cooler, I asked permission to hunt the grouse and he said, "What the hell, I never eat the damn things. Go ahead."

Opening the rickety post-and-barbed-wire gate, I managed to inflict only minor bloodshed on my wrists and hands. The rancher shook his head and went back to work.

The birds were farther than they'd seemed, more than a half-mile up over a deceptively steep rise through thick sage and up onto a small bench. The grouse were still visible and acted like nothing was wrong. Already warm from the walk, I shed my sweater, leaving it to dry on a tall bush. Outside of hunting chukar or sharptails (or perhaps ruffed grouse or pheasant or maybe blues), sage grouse demand the most physical exertion. I was reminded of another hunt last season out in the coulees south of Miles City....

That day was not warm —it was hot, and the little water my friend and I carried was gone. He was somewhere ahead and to my right looking for the birds in a small draw. I was sitting on a flat rock baking my brains to a fine turn.

Playing with a stick in the dust to kill some time before this would all be over and I could enjoy a cold drink and a warm fire in the cooling dusk, I watched an army of small red ants wreak havoc with a column of outnumbered, less-aggressive black ants. The carnage was awful. Black ants were writhing on the ground covered by the mean red ones or they were being dragged off as potential food or slave labor. The massacre lasted for a few minutes, then they were all gone, dead and living alike.

A few grasshoppers made half-hearted attempts at flight, clacking and crashing into the brittle grass and against the tan rocks. A spider looked cooked in its web in front of me in the weeds. The body was crinkled, burnt.

Harsh land. How could there be birds here, even well-adapted sage grouse. And then I heard two shots and watched as a grouse dropped in the draw not far away. The air was still moving up slope with the heat, and a half dozen grouse rounded a knob and came straight at me.

Standing as quickly as a heatstroked body would allow, I fired at the lead bird, a big sucker, and missed. The second shot hit the sage grouse as he started to rise over me and he splashed into the white, chalky soil behind, sending up a plume of dust that dissipated on the breeze. The rest of the birds vanished over a hill we'd labored up over an hour before. They were safe. Our truck was in the other direction, and I was beat and very thirsty.

That was the extent of that day's work, and yet for some reason it remains crystal clear in my mind. The sharp relief of the flats and the rock formations. The perfume of sage in the heat; the slight sensation of dizziness; the overriding feeling that I should pick up the grouse and stagger back to the rig. The hunt was over....

Now, watching the still-oblivious grouse as I moved closer, I wondered if today would be like that one. Eighty degrees and dressed for fifty. Upland bird hunting with sweat-soaked shadings.

Now within forty yards and still no activity. Were these well-crafted decoys (sage grouse decoys?) planted by the rancher to humble burned-out road bums?

Then beating wings flashed everywhere. The first shot dropped a bird to the ground just over there by a bunch of sage. The other blast shredded the air, and the birds climbed the next rise with rapidly thrashing wings interrupted briefly by swift glides angling tight to the earth.

Like always, the shooting ended in a second and was scratched into an addled mind forever. The grouse was flapping its wings and flopping on the ground as I approached. Swinging it by the neck in tight circles ended the bird's struggles, a big male, over seven pounds by the heft as I weighed it in my hand. The body felt cool through the thick feathers.

Retrieving the sweater, I crawled through the gate this time, forsaking more bloodshed. The rancher looked up from his ditch and nodded, barely. I waved, field-dressed the sage hen, wrapped it in a plastic bag, and dropped it in the cooler alongside a melting chunk of block ice.

Turning back on the highway was uneventful, probably disappointing to the rancher.

Still 300 miles from home, but a nice way to end an extended stretch of road time.

Chapter Two

Hungarian Partridge

The first time I shot a Hun, I was chasing sharptails, but that's how things often go in my bird hunting, flyfishing, and day-to-day peregrinations. What happens, happens; there's no point in getting too worked up about the unexpected.

I was pushing up through a tight draw of tall grass, thick brush, and hidden varmint entrances with my friend, "the Big Tall Dummy." Our knees and ankles were wrenched and stretched from the unpredictable footing, and we were a little warm and out of breath. It was a pleasant afternoon during the first week of September. The upland bird season opened three days back and this was our first day out. Way out. Up along the Hi-Line north of Chinook in rolling country that fell apart here and there, forming rough little coulees and crisp breaks that dropped down steadily on the sides of marginal stream courses all the way from the Canadian border some miles north. Prime country for sharptails.

The road in here was a winner that didn't have the decency to live up to its reputation (according to advanced billing on the map, anyway) of being graded gravel. Well, to be fair, the bugger was civil to us for a few miles, but after no time, the gravel was gone, replaced by ruts and grooves that must prove fine sport when conditions are wet. Gumbo city and a hundred bucks to the nearest rancher willing to fire up his tractor. I'd been there before, all over Montana. Triple A won't visit in the boonies.

At any rate, after bouncing and careering along the road at forty miles an hour for three or four months, we came to the green gate with the battered sign that must have advertised some sort of grain years ago. The metal was shot up and rusted now. We'd start on the other side of the thing.

A phone call to a number gleaned from a friend of a friend over whiskey late one weekday night at The Flame bar in Missoula secured permission to hunt a couple of days on a couple of dozen sections of wheat, native grass, and CRP land. We stopped at the owner's house back by town, dodged some feisty yard dogs, banged on the door, introduced ourselves, handed over a bottle of Old Grand Dad (more late night ammunition), asked directions, and now we were at the green gate.

The country looked like prime sharptail habitat, even to my neophyte eyes of so many years ago. Plenty of feed in the fields and tight draws with thick brush cover mere yards away — easy eating and quick shelter from predators and marauding weather.

My friend turned loose his Irish setter, a hunting dog only in name. Training and discipline were not part of the Big Tall Dummy's routine. He'd passed these aversions on to Rusty, the dog taking to the easy, carefree life like a natural. The setter pushed up birds in each of the first four draws and the fields above. Lots of them, in pairs and groups of five or more. Too bad he was at least a quarter-mile ahead. My 870 Wingmaster was dependable, but 2 ¾ 6s were out of their league with this action.

Finally, Rusty ran out of gas, collapsing on the edge of a field, tongue hanging way out and eyes slightly bugged. We caught up and prodded him to foot. Winding sidelong to the bottom of the drainage, we worked up a narrow cut of grass and small bunches of brush. Seven or eight sharps jumped up in front of Rusty who was only twenty yards ahead. Must be a lot of birds here to be gathered together so early, or maybe nobody hunted them. We both shot and dropped three; one-and-a-half each we decided in youthful diplomacy. We worked on up some more and finished off the singles and filled our limit, game pouches hanging wonderfully full on our rear ends. A great time. Easy shooting. Time for a beer and finding a motel room. Tomorrow we'd limit out early and head home. Our work was done here for today.

Or so we thought.

Rusty was into the game now and working well. It was like someone from far above had thrown a switch and the lights went blazing on behind his eyes. The dim bulb that was Rusty- the-hunter was now quartz-halogen Rusty-the-bird dog. Back and forth, methodically and close in, when feathered craziness blew up in our faces.

A dozen smallish, gray birds blasted up in all directions, squawking something that sounded like a chorus of people chirping, "*Wheat for you.*"

"They're Huns, Holt," and the Big Tall Dummy was already firing as he spoke.

"What the hell," I thought. "Where's the first tee and what's the course record?" and I shot and pumped the 870 as fast as I could. There was gunfire all over the place. Birds were buzzing, diving, and circling in mad dashes like a World War I dogfight choreographed by Mel Brooks. Smoke choked the wind, smelling acrid and sweet.

"How can two people make so much noise and only drop two birds?" I asked myself as the mayhem subsided. The remaining Huns escaped over the ridge to the next draw, and they did this quickly. With dispatch. They were gone.

Rusty retrieved both birds smartly. There'd be no living with the dog in town. He'd probably want to sip some Scotch and watch the nightly news.

The Hun I'd hit was small, fitting nicely in the palm of my hand, but the bird was solid, muscular. A light-brown mask covered his throat and shaded back around the now-dimming eyes. Most of the body was gray with flecks of dark brown in the wings and scattered through the short tail feathers.

What a neat little bird. I wanted more.

Walking back the way we came and starting up the next cut in the land, Rusty moved farther ahead and the birds flushed madly. Another salvo and one more bird. Wild, frenetic shooting one more time.

This was great sport. I really wanted more, but the light was fading.

"Tomorrow, an early start. Fill out on the grouse and then let's get after these Huns."

"That means getting up before noon, Holt," riposted the dummy with a seven-foot-tall grin. "Remember those words later when you reach for the Beam."

Well, we made it early, though a little rumpled, and we shot sharps, but saw no more Huns. I've been hooked on those birds ever since.

Toward the end of September, I met Chuck and Blanche Johnson in the grassy, tree-shrouded parking lot of a small group of cottages just north of East Glacier on the edge of the Blackfeet Indian Reservation. We planned to meet up with tribal member and my good friend Joe Kipp tomorrow morning to hunt Huns in his country. After unloading our gear, my friends followed me out to Four Horns Lake for a bit of late-season trout action. The two-laned ruts into the large lake were dry but entertaining. The wind was howling winter as it whipped the sapphire water into an ugly mood.

We rigged up and I wandered off to fish a small bay. Snow was driving down from the lowering, darkening sky. I took two nice rainbows of five pounds or so in a hurry on an olive-and-black woolly bugger. The trout were fat and shining red and hammered silver in the dull light. I bumped a few more without hooking up. I could see Chuck pumping on a keg of Black Bart Stout given to me by the owner of Whitefish Brewing, Gary Hutchinson, a good guy who'd survived some hard times and knew how to make a hell of a beer. If my companions had forsaken flyfishing for stout, the storm must be worse than I realized.

I reached our vehicles in what was now a driving blizzard. I crawled out of my waders and started back to pavement and sanity. Only two-wheel drive, the Toyota was airborne and sideways and sliding all over the greasy mud and slippery grass. The highway finally showed up. There was only a dented muffler to show for some of the most exciting road work I'd ever participated in. Later, back at the rooms, we burned some steaks on a grill outside in the snow and talked away the night.

A good start.

Joe was awake early the next morning when I called from a phone booth down the road. Snow covered the ground and the day looked surly. He said he'd be waiting, and I saw a bear amble off behind our cabins. Nothing new. Bears are part of the state and common around East Glacier, especially after the tourists go back home.

Thirty minutes later we pulled off a breezy bench and down a rocky road to Joe's place nestled in the cottonwoods along a small creek. A nice spot and, as he said last summer, "John, all I can say is it's out of the wind."

You had to live along the Rocky Mountain Front to appreciate those words. I'd watched the wind flatten lakes and send up miniature water spouts many times. Mobile homes are blown apart and away each year. People park their cars so that the windshields are sheltered from the full force of the near-constant gales. The wind, always the damn wind, is as much a part of this land as the countless acres of wild grasses that seem to flow like a wide river in the rushing air.

Bird hunting is interesting in these conditions. Huns get up and vanish like a bright idea conjured half-awake at 3 a.m.

We drove miles into the center of rolling, hilly country that seemed deserted despite the obvious agrarian attentions paid to it by ranchers during the year. We hunted up and down meandering, spacious draws, Chuck and Blanche's two German wirehairs, Cody and dear sweet Annie, working like maniacs in the thick fields. The year was running late and the fields of wheat were still standing.

Finding Huns was going to be a bitch. The grain was up to our shoulders. You could hide a woolly mammoth in there.

Giving up, we went to another location along a wandering stream guarded by steep cutbanks of dark, coal-like rock. Dense wetlands gave way to more open country in the north. Still no birds, not even a sharp, and we'd walked a lot and were tired. Back at the truck the keg of Black Bart took several serious hits. The strong brew revived our sagging energy reserves. The keg took another round without flinching. Bibulous behavior was dancing on the near soft-blue northwest horizon.

"Stop talking. Listen. What's that sound? Huns coming down that rise?" asked Kipp.

We all turned silent, listening with serious intent. It was true. The birds were coming right at us. Shotguns appeared out of nowhere. Crouching, stalking visages fanned out from the trucks. This was it.

"The thing is they sounded a lot like sandhill cranes and they sounded far off," but I'd displayed such consistent confusion already on the trip, nobody listened. We moved cautiously forward.

Then Kipp said, "John's right," with a laugh and he pointed at a couple of dozen sandhills winging it toward the southeast. He shrugged and jived, "Even a damn writer gets it right once in awhile."

That was the end of that hunt. The day ended with large steaks at a restaurant near the summit of Marias Pass. Chuck and Blanche drove to the cabins. I stayed at Joe's bunkhouse, talking about his involvement with his people's problems and issues — hard, honest truths and histories I was unaware of and honored to be a small part of, if only through the listening. Straight talk kept among friends. Joe's one of the best. I'll hunt and fish with him anywhere.

There was a hard frost on the ground the next morning as we drove off to the far northeast corner of the reservation. The sun was just above the horizon and blazing atomic orange. You could tell it would be hot by early afternoon. We rolled through river bottoms torched by the yellow-gold of turning cottonwoods. Salmon-colored road dust hung in a long trail behind us as we raced along before turning onto cracked pavement, then off through a stretch of wild grass, climbing all the way to the top of a ridge that looked like nothing until you hopped out of the truck and looked over the edge. This is where we'd hunt.

I tripped, stumbled, and skied to the bottom through more chokecherry and high brush. Chuck worked the middle. Blanche and Joe walked on top. Hundreds of feet of rock outcropping roared above, home to nesting eagles earlier in the year. The dogs and Chuck and I had a hard time of it. There were animal burrows hiding in the undergrowth. The dogs' bells clanged ahead of us somewhere, out of sight. If Huns did surface, the shooting would be difficult. We'd be swinging on them as they rode the embryonic thermals to safety. Balance was an issue, even standing still. We worked a mile without turning anything. The climb up —short, pumping steps assisted by handholds on the bushes — was a killer. Chuck and I were more than out of breath when we reached the ridgeline, and the day was just heating up. Kipp was waiting for us, laughing something about "getting revenge on white men." He had.

Only 11 a.m. I needed a gun bearer.

Striking off into even more isolated country just a football field short of the Canadian border, Joe pointed out a lake that held buffalo stones, a species of dinosaur only inches long, beneath its bed. Hard to visualize tiny reptiles scampering about on this now-arid land that was once ocean-swamp. Farther away he indicated a large butte where he claimed St. Elmo's Fire used to zing and sizzle.

"Around the base and out across the lower slopes," he said. "The fire's gone now. I haven't seen it in years. It disappeared for a reason," and he looked at me with a stare that said more than I think I needed to feel. Joe is the first to downplay the image of his people as mystical beings imbued with an otherworldly knowledge we non-tribal members can only imagine. He does believe that living on the plains for thousands of years has given the Blackfeet an awareness that goes far behind what the casual visitor experiences.

Joe believes in preserving the "old ways," spreading this wisdom among his people. And he has shared some of this with me in confidence. I'm not being coy; it's just that Joe and I have slowly established a solid trust and friendship over the years, one we both value. I only mention these things as a way of explaining why his land is special to me, close to the heart. I came to Montana years ago because of my feelings for the land. The stories Joe tells make the attachment stronger, small roots I never expected to have. Telling things he asked me not to would be a betrayal, selfish. That's all.

We finally topped a rise that gave way to vistas that rolled far into Alberta's wheat fields and rose-colored soil. Distant bluffs betrayed the presence of the Milk River. The three main buttes of the Sweetgrass Hills shimmered in the east, capped in new-fallen snow. The Front dominated the west. Coulees and bluffs ran away forever to the south.

God! I could hunt here forever, never turning a bird, and be satisfied, at peace.

The dogs were eager and we all worked hard without success. I climbed up on top of a bluff carpeted with gray and buff grass. I could see Blanche, Chuck, and the dogs moving slowly far below. Joe was on another ridge farther away.

Instantly, a big bunch of sharptails burst around my feet, scaring the hell out of me. My heart nearly exploded and I wanted to shoot, but held back. Non-tribal members could only hunt Huns — other species were off limits. Too bad. Joe was trying to persuade the tribal council to change its thinking. His people are beginning to realize the value of sportsmen's dollars. The area's trophy rainbow fishery is already bringing in much-needed money.

The day rolled on serene, perfect. No clouds. A touch of breeze. In the seventies. And no Huns. One very well-fed mule deer spooked at our approach and barely made it over a fence, almost falling down with the burden of its weight. I sympathized with the animal's situation.

Two days and no Huns, but we all had a fine time. I'd meet up with Chuck and Blanche in November to hunt pheasants near Lewistown. For now it was good-bye and time to cruise back over Marias Pass down the Middle Fork of the Flathead River and home to Whitefish.

Much walking and no birds. That, too, is what hunting Hungarian partridge is about. If birds are more important than good country, best to chase pheasants or sharptails. They're more dependable overall. Days spent afield with good people in unspoiled country — that should be enough.

One of the misconceptions concerning Huns is that they fly so much faster than sharptails. They do get up to form quicker, but the two species' relative speeds are similar. Sharps, being stronger, tend to get out of thick cover faster. The smaller size of the Huns creates the illusion, especially since it is not uncommon to see both birds rise from the same cover. Huns, having relatively few blood vessels in their breast muscles (unlike, say, sage grouse) tend to tire after several flushes.

When wounded slightly and not immediately retrieved, they will cover amazing ground. On a recent trip, a member of our party dropped a Hun that did its patented disappearing act into thick cover. Our dogs were unable to locate the creature. When returning back down the creekbed at the end of the day, one of the dogs became birdy. The Hun made a crippled leap for freedom, but was snared by the leaping hound. This was a quarter-of-a-mile away from where it had been shot earlier.

In addition to draws and creek bottoms, old, abandoned ranch buildings and decaying homesteads are excellent locations. I've seen a covey running around one such place in central Montana every time I've hunted the property. They amble about like avian royalty regally ensconced in their domain of secure shelter and ample food supply of volunteer grains. Trying to flush the birds without a dog has proved futile. They easily run and hide in the nooks and crannies of the old structures.

Hunting with a friend and his yellow Lab turned the trick one season. The dog worked aggressively inside an old shed and the Huns came barreling out of a window opening like respected businessmen fleeing a raided whorehouse. The two of us both happened to be positioned near the window and we each managed to double (a rarity for me). The Lab flushed the singles and we took a few more without finishing off the covey, leaving a number of seed birds for next season.

When the birds are feeding, they seem to be hyper-alert and difficult to approach. This holds form even near dark. When they're hunkered down in cover or loafing, their radar seems to be turned down. They may be hard to locate in the thickets, but you can work in for a decent shot.

The same shooting can be found around grain bins, but popping a bunch of holes in the metal canister is not advised. Farmers find this to be something of an annoyance.

Commonly associated with the 4,000- to 5,000-foot elevations of the plains, the birds can be found on the high benches and snow slopes thousands of feet higher, even in the cold of November. Friends near Deer Lodge say they find more Huns in these spots than down in the more climatically forgiving valley where food is abundant, surmising that the coveys have fled the more heavily populated and hunted lowlands.

When first flushed, a covey often breaks as a group, flying briefly in one direction, then vectoring sharply in another, rarely flying more than a few hundred yards the first time up. Often when approached, the Huns actually move to more open ground, no doubt to gain a better view of what's going down. There have been places where I have found the coveys to flush in the same direction and for the same duration each season. Whether this is some form of genetic imprinting, I'm not sure, but the behavior certainly helps cut down on the legwork.

Another tactic, if you are familiar with the country you are working, is to flush the birds and then carefully work over the hill they fled behind, hopefully into the wind. At the top be prepared to find birds moving unconcernedly near the crest. They probably figure they've eluded whatever scared them to death in the first place.

Because Hungarian partridge (*Perdix perdix* to be precise) are native to Eurasia and relatively recent introductions to the West, many farmers and ranchers refer to them by all sorts of misnomers including quail and, according to John Barsness in his book *Hunting The Great Plains*, blue ruffed grouse, which actually would make an intriguing hybrid, all things considered. Huns are found in much of the same country as sage grouse and in portions of northern Nevada and even in western Minnesota, northwestern Iowa, southwestern Manitoba, and much of Saskatchewan. The populations of the Northwest are probably the result of Alberta plantings that gradually migrated southward. Introductions east of the Mississippi have not proved wildly successful.

Huns pair up as early as February and the hatching season is usually late spring, though they can be on their nests in early summer. It is not uncommon for a hen to nest a second time, and by October the hunter may come across adults and two age classes of the year. Hens can lay as many as twenty eggs in the ground-based nest that is found near a water source. Early in the season, coveys run around a dozen birds, but as the season progresses, these groups join forces to form large flocks that may still be defined by the original family units.

One of the more curious sights I've stumbled across is a circle in the snow formed by the tailfeathers and feet of the Huns with their small, pellet-like droppings forming a smaller circle inside. The birds nest this way for warmth and to some extent protection from predators, but I would imagine, viewed from above, this circle would appear more like a target to a hawk or falcon. A sumptuous vision worth aiming for.

Like most upland species, Huns are a boom-and-bust bird. One year they are everywhere you have hunted them in the past, the next they're almost non-existent. Cold, wet springs and drought are the main causes of population cycle downturns, but numbers of predators also rise with increased numbers of birds in synchronous fashion. In seasons of low ebb, hunting places that produced before is sound strategy. Even with this knowledge, finding Huns without a dog borders on futile in most cases. Once alerted, the birds immediately slip away into impenetrable cover like thickets of wild roses or buffaloberry. Truly high sport if you like ripped pants, torn shooting gloves, and bloodied hands without the added inconvenience of shooting and retrieving partridge.

Almost any breed is better than no dog, but pointers seem to work the best, though a flushing dog that works close-in can be enjoyable.

Huns also take advantage of snow, flying into snowbanks to elude pursuit or using the snow for cover from the weather. Other factors to consider are that they often seek gravel and dirt roads for grit in late afternoon. This, unfortunately, draws road hunters that blast the poor birds, guns malevolently aimed through rolled-down windows of their still-running pickups. A truly fine breed of human. Also, when separated from the main group, lone birds will utter a screechy, squeaky call, one I was clueless about until a more-experienced friend pointed the sound out to me one October outing. This call is rarely made before the cover of dusk.

The Sweetgrass Hills rise up out of the starkness of the Hi-Line along the U.S.-Canadian border like three little volcanoes. The highest reaches of these miniature mountain ranges rise more than 3,000 feet above the prairie that rolls off in all directions for miles. Formed by igneous intrusion fifty million years ago, they are visible from fifty or more miles away, from places like Choteau in the south, Conrad to the east, and Browning in the west. In the spring, fields of wheat and canola carpet the flatlands in brilliant greens and blazing yellow.

Even driving by them on U.S. 2, the hills exert a magnetic pull. They look powerful and majestic. They are the dominant land-mark in this part of Montana. It seems that no matter how far you drive or in what direction, the Sweetgrass are always there, loom-ing silently above all, ghostly in the haze of a hot summer after-noon, eerily beautiful with fresh snow in early autumn.

The Blackfeet consider them sacred, a source of power and spiritual inspiration. The grasses that grow here are part of their rit-uals. Tribal members spend days in fasting and on vision quests; or they bake in the darkness of sweat lodges filled with an atmos-phere of smoldering native plants, steam, and sweat.

Elk migrate across the plains from near the Rocky Mountain Front to feast on the abundance of luxuriant grass. Mule and whitetail deer abound in the region. Canada and snow geese along with tundra swans and mallards pass through each spring and fall. There are ruffed and blue grouse in the timber higher up. And there are pheasants and sharptails and Huns. This may be the best country for the small birds in the state.

The Hills have always intrigued me. For years I drove past them wondering what secrets they held. Were there small streams tumbling down through the pine forests? Or perhaps high lakes or ranch ponds filled with huge trout? Or were there upland birds in staggering numbers?

Finally one May, after years of procrastination, I decided to find out. In search of a small lake reputed to hold trout, I wan-dered aimlessly on the dusty backroads that twist and weave through the hills. I drove the old pickup, checking out the country from West Butte over to Gold Butte and then well lost up to the tiny town of Whitlash and farther north to the border and the Port of Whitlash and then on back the way I came, then over to the rolling hills and billiard table-level benches beneath Mt. Brown.

I stopped every so often and smoked a small cigar, a way of slowing my head down from the pace of the road and examining the land. The views were awe-inspiring. Not like the vertical splendor of Glacier National Park nor the Beartooth Mountains, but in a more subtle, yet powerful, way.

This was magic country. I could feel the hills running through me, making me feel insignificant, less than nothing. A joyous experience jammed with a sense of freedom so strong, so tangible, I found myself laughing and babbling away to the tune of "Holy shit! Look at the color of the grass. Damn. There went a muley buck. Look at all the water."

After stopping and asking directions at various ranches from people that were all far older than I, the pond in question turned out to be just over a series of rises I had ignored for the first seventy hours of misdirected navigation. As I crossed a tiny creek, a Hun hen and her brood of a dozen chicks zipped across the road in front of me. The young ones were the size of cue balls, fuzzy and oblivious to anything beyond the bouncing tail of the bird directly in front. Turning up a path coursing along the side of one of the hills, I spotted two more broods. Then several more as I wound past the scars of an abandoned placer gold-mining operation. Reaching the pond, I saw another batch, and there were Canadas cruising the far shore. Several antelope were glowing farther away in the orange light of sunset.

Just behind where I would pitch the tent, several ponds blending into marsh attracted ducks by the dozens. They came circling out of the sky in dark vees framed by the sun. Huge holes tunneled into the side of the raised two-track path indicated badgers. Trout were rising all over the pond. Lengthening shadows turned velvet purple.

I sure as hell could see why the Blackfeet held this place in high esteem. My two-plus days there were a quick taste of paradise. No people, though there were signs that anglers and hunters from Shelby and maybe Great Falls played here on occasion. The trout were suicidal. I caught big ones in the dark, beneath the stars. Sometimes the fly never hit the water as the rainbows churned the surface to a froth for one bizarre hour before a madman of a storm powered through, venting its energy in intense lightning and deafening thunder, finally bombing the ground, the truck, the tent, and me senseless with hail that was, thank God, only the size of marbles. In the morning the air was thick with the scent of sage and, of course, sweet grass, grass that was waving gently in a soft breeze below a dark blue sky.

I'd be back in the fall for the Huns. One of the ranchers I spoke with said I could hunt here. I'd bring along some bourbon (I'd noticed that there was a half-full bottle sitting on the kitchen table). And I'd bring a jar of Lynda's huckleberry jam. One can't be too careful about these things.

The first week of October found me on the front stoop of the rancher's home (I'd found the place on the second try). Bottle of Jim Beam in one hand, jam in the other. I put on my best aluminum siding salesman smile and prayed the guy would remember me from this spring and prayed harder still that access was still there for the asking.

The wood door opened and the rancher appeared, blurred slightly by the screen door still between us. He opened that door and stepped out. I stepped back. He was wearing beat-up cowboy boots, faded jeans, and a tattered flannel shirt — old-time Montana for sure.

"Back again. After those birds I expect." He'd remembered and I handed him the offerings.

"Didn't have to, but thanks. Come on in and we'll have a little. I'm Jim." I introduced myself and we shook hands, his a rough, long-fingered one with a hard grip.

We walked through a living room that was also Montana. New and old sofas, recliners, and footstools. Hardwood flooring. Throw rugs. Family photos arranged on top of a television that was off. Pictures of bull and bronc riders on the walls. Coveralls and jackets scattered about. Two rifles and a shotgun leaning in a corner. Country on the radio in the kitchen. Linoleum floor and the tableclothed table. I sat in the chair he indicated. A Winston was smoldering in a filled ashtray, a nearly empty pack beside it. Two tall glasses appeared. Jim sat down, twisting the top open and pouring booze in a fluid motion. Several ounces each and he downed his in one pull.

"Oh, shit," I thought. This could be trouble, and I did the same without too much fuss.

"Another?"

"Sure."

And so it went and I barely remember Jim writing on the back of a flyer promoting Senator Max Baucus as the next great statesman. And I remember a bit less about driving the little road that wound through the browning grasses to a campsite up on a high flat overlooking the country. And I remember nothing about going to sleep in the bag on top of the crumpled tarp pitched on the ground far from the truck.

The sun woke me and I was thirsty. Terribly so. Them old dehydration blues, again. The Baucus map was jammed in my shirt pocket. I felt like hell, but at least I was hurting in good country.

A few yards beyond the truck a small spring trickled clear water down into a tiny pool. I stripped. Stern measures were required. Immediately cold, I sank to my knees by the flow. Genuflection before the open spaces to the great deity, Self-abuse. My heart flip-flopped as the icy water washed over my head and down my back. The skin where it was tanned from a summer out-side turned darker brown with reddish-copper tones. The rest of my body, a dapper pale white, flushed hot pink. Stepping back, I let the morning wind dry me and then grabbed a handful of sage leaves and rubbed them along my arms. Less than twenty-four hours from home, and Holt's gone native.

Curious doings then. In the corner of an edge of my vision I sensed movement. Dancing, stick-like figures the color of the night sky moved herky-jerky between two of the buttes. I turned and faced them head on. They weren't there. The silly things were rocking around just on the fringe of my sight. They vanished as I turned. Again and again for the longest time. Perhaps this was a skin-contact, sagebrush high.

After awhile the things left me alone, but there was strange electricity in the air. I could feel it running along my arms and down my spine. I knew I was crazy. Everybody did, but what a place to go benignly bananas. Worse things have happened.

Dressing quickly, I was soon feeling warm, by recent comparison, and comfortable. Taking the high road, I opted for some orange juice and a bagel with cream cheese.

The big-game season was a couple of weeks off. Maybe the hills and draws around here would be empty. Mine alone.

The stock ponds and small reservoirs shone silver and orange in the morning light as the sun topped the hills rising hundreds of feet above. In the clean air, West Butte appeared so near, it looked touchable, an arm's length away. I could see cattle in the valley below and a tractor was moving determinedly across a half-turned field, soundless up here. Once the boots were on, I checked pockets for shells, grabbed the 20-gauge, and began working down to the base of a grassy draw that Jim said (according to his map) held plenty of Huns. The wind was quartering but I figured I smelled like sage. I was invisible. Ralph Ellison, Montana style.

A couple of hundred yards of forced march through the unyielding grass and I was warm. A few more minutes of walking, and the feeling that birds were near hit me, that unexplained predatorial sense that I wish I had a lot more of. And then the Huns were in my face. Firing wildly, I managed to miss them all as they tore across the ridge to the north. A few minutes to calm down and let the birds regroup, and I was off, not able to resist the urge any longer to find them and shoot a couple.

It is amazing what a healthy shot of adrenaline can do to ameliorate the effects of a late night. Veins and surface capillaries are flushed clean, and good red blood flows like pure fire.

Working slowly to the edge of the rise and peering over the top of a pile of rock and dying grass, I saw the Huns. They were just puttering around in odd little patterns, unconcerned.

Might as well go in without knocking. Up they went, and I rolled one and drew tailfeathers on another. The birds soared up and over the next hill, really going this time. I had all day and started after them. As I started up this draw, more birds, a different covey, took off and I hit another and missed with the second. Hell, this was almost like Phil Harris and Curt Gowdy doing their thing on the long-dead *American Sportsman* television show of the sixties. Two Huns in less than an hour. Onward and upward for more.

The wind had died by the time I reached the spot where I thought the birds had landed. Open ground surrounded by large tracts of thick, tall grass. Where was the dog? Where were the beaters? No way, but walking a touch farther, several more Huns from one of the coveys rose and one more pinwheeled into the grass. Twenty minutes of thrashing about to find the bird was enough for this morning.

Ten o'clock. Noon somewhere on the planet. Time for a small fire, a couple of Huns, maybe a sliced pear and a few beers. If only things could be so easy all of the time. But if they were, just like in flyfishing, the excitement and wonder would dissipate like smoke on the wind. Being humbled and confused is part of the hunt, too. The next day-and-a-half would no doubt reinforce that concept.

The morning had turned flat-out spectacular. Warm. A few clouds. The Sweetgrass Hills were radiant; there's no other way to put things.

A perfect time. All by myself, feeling satisfied, a bit cocky, and just lonely enough to want to hide out here forever.

Chapter Three

Chukar

"I don't much care for those birds at all. You walk straight up some of the meanest country around, and the damn birds fly straight down right by your knees. Never have had a decent shot. It's too tough for me," and that was the end of that conversation. My Bridger, Montana chukar connection dried up in the withering heat of his personal failure.

I hung up the phone and realized that once again I'd be on my own, wandering half lost without defensible purpose, and for what? Goofy chukars. Birds about the size of ruffed grouse that live in arid, broken, rocky, sheer country at the end of no place special.

Every time I think about chukars and ponder why I ever hunt them to begin with, I realize that, if anything, chasing this bird is probably as accurate a metaphor for my life as anything — hard to find, difficult to deal with, and isolated by nature. Hunting these unique birds is in some ways the practice of the skillful art of hiding out in country given up for beyond dead, considered more like just plain worthless by most normal people. Conventional society, God rest its mediocre soul, could care less about these attributes, now finely honed by years of practice. Hunting chukars, like savoring a good cigar or flyfishing in February or not voting in local elections, is an acquired taste. One that only tastes sweeter, in a slightly perverse way, with the passage of many confused years. Thankfully, few people enjoy these arcane pleasures. Solitude. Don't take my damned *solitude*.

No wonder I love chukars. It sure can't be because they are easy to find, let alone hit with anything bordering on a fifty-percent success rate. Try twenty on a good day.

A long time ago when things were simple and I was pretending to go to college, spare time was most of the time. Running down the Interstate from Missoula bound for the desert-like country miles east of Bridger, itself several hundred miles distant, was a piece of cake. No big deal. Knowing little about chukars, other than what I'd heard in sport shops and from friends who'd lived in Montana all their lives, I spent a lot of time trying to find the birds. Sometimes I did, or rather my hound did.

I may be the only person to ever hunt chukar with an Irish wolfhound. A good friend and eager traveler, Bonzo (named after the Irish group Bonzo Dog Band who authored the seminal work *Tubas in the Moonlight*) took to the sport with an enthusiasm untempered by the knowledge that his was a breed far more suited to running coyotes or, as Colonel Gallatin did more than a century ago, elk. Bonzo was a happy guy who saw more mystery in life, and in the smallest of things, than all but a very few people I've known, and these few are all dear friends.

We'd wind our way far into the hills that crinkled and bunched up east of the Clarks Fork of the Yellowstone River. The Toyota Landcruiser (another one of "them damn foreign rigs") was ideally suited to the rough terrain. Hot Tuna or the Allman Brothers or perhaps It's A Beautiful Day blasted from the eight-track as we jounced blindly into the center of oblivion. We didn't have a clue where we were headed or what we were doing, even after we'd been where we were going a few times.

The waitress and some ranchers at a cafe in Bridger suggested where we might find some birds, but they thought the whole scheme was, if not absurd, certainly laughable.

"Why the hell would you want to hunt wild chickens?" they asked.

"Sounds like fun," I replied. "And I've never shot any before."

"Probably won't this time, either. And if it rains, you'll be in there 'til things dry off in May. But don't worry — you won't last that long. Hope you got a dog."

And I pointed out the cafe windows to my hound, lounging in the front seat, his head as big as a horse's.

"Oh, Jesus," one of them said, and they all cracked up. It was funny and I laughed, too, all the while wondering if this might be the same sort of mistake that family and friends had seen me make with a degree of consistency that would have astounded any statistician keeping records on such things.

"Good luck," and they meant it." Check back in. We want to hear about this one."

So we were barreling along on a high plateau looking for where we had been directed, and the rocky bluffs pulled into view. Treeless. Barren. Real empty-looking. Ten gallons of water. A red gerry can of spare gas. Plenty of food, beer, and a little bourbon. No wood, just rock-hard brush for fires. This was it.

Setting up camp, such as it was, was routine. I did the work and Bonzo found an elevated spot to stare off into eternity. Gaze hounds. A great breed, but what do they see? What are they thinking?

I had no idea if Bonzo would or even could flush anything. I only hoped so. We struck off to the pile of rocks that grew in stature as they came closer. They initially appeared to be only a mile off. Try three or four. The ground was uneven and spiked with nasty clumps of low-level cactus. The hound got stuck once and didn't like it. I pulled out the spines and he never did bump into the stuff again. College material.

The 200-foot elevations seen from the Landcruiser expanded to hundreds, possibly a thousand feet in places. The chukar were up there. That's what we'd been told in town. Maybe we could ground-sluice some rattlesnakes. I was afraid of heights. We started up.

The huge scale of this land had some advantages. The closer in, the more apparent the openings, game trails, and flat stretches became. If the birds were near this country, we could shoot at them. Still, some of the walking turned into a vertical scramble and I never looked down. If I did, I'd fall and that would hurt.

"What happened to Holt, that worthless piece of crap?"

"He died falling off a cliff somewhere in Montana chasing chukars."

"Chukars?"

"Some kind of wild bird."

"Who found him?"

"Some Indians out there I guess. That big dog of his wouldn't let anyone near what was left. He's still out there. So's the dog."

"Figures."

The dog stayed close, perhaps a bit intimidated by this country, as I was. Normally he ranged well in front of me, only to come loping back an hour or so later like he'd never been gone. He soon was nosing about the rocks and into the thick brush, pausing now and then to watch "master"laboring up behind him, muttering strikingly inventive strings of multihyphenated obscenities.

Finally reaching level ground, a place to catch my breath, I heard a chorus *chuka-rrrrs* from a jumble of rock and dry grass. Perhaps my cafe friends were playing a joke, but no. The dog leaped forward, backward, sideways, and up (sounds like an old Yardbirds' album) simultaneously, and a covey of birds I'd never seen before rocketed up as one, then screamed down at me like a squadron of MIG 21s. I shot out of shock, possibly instinct. Raising my gun (a Remington Model 32 that I wish I hadn't sold for quick cash later on) and firing twice before the stock reached shoulder height, I dropped a bird. I'm not sure with which shot. I wasn't tracking anything in particular.

Bonzo ran over and sniffed the fallen bird that looked a lot like photographs I'd seen of chukars. Native to the region or not, they were remarkable to look at. Sort of like quail without the tuft on the head. Sandy-colored across the chest and back, flanks barred black and white, a white throat and a black necklace curving down to just below the throat, a red bill and matching legs, a designer game bird for an addled hipster — a bird from another planet. This seemed appropriate considering where we were looked like Mars.

I didn't mark the others, but assumed they tucked into similar cover down below. The hound was into this now. I think most hunting species, whatever they're bred for, pick up on these things to some extent.

The way back was circuitous, steep, and long, turning knees rubbery. Bonzo kicked up two more, and I missed both as they dove down and then out and around the base of the rock formation. I lost sight of each when I brought my barrel down on the birds, no doubt shooting a half-dozen feet over and behind the chukars.

The others from the covey failed to materialize again. It was past five and the sun, even in early October, was heading down. Time to water and feed the hound, clean the chukar, gather some brush, build a drink, and cook some food.

Why would any sane person spend day after day in a classroom learning brain-dead jive when he could be out here in this undisciplined land chasing lunatic chukars? In one of those rare moments of clarity and prescience, I realized that my college career was damn near a dead issue. Making my way was not going to be easy, but I sure wasn't going to blow any more time sitting in a room full of posturing B.S. artists sucking up to grade-B clowns masquerading as educators (to be fair, I did encounter some fine teachers during my whirlwind tour of academia) too afraid of the real world to get their butts off campus and play a little hardball. I'd learned enough at college(s) to know I'd had enough. I wanted out, but I digress.

Bonzo drank a half-gallon of water and chomped down five pounds of chicken necks (his favorite food), then dug a fairly feeble nest in some grass not far from where I was building a small fire pit. A little scrounging turned up enough wood for the evening's downscale fire, which torched nicely with only one match and a few ounces of charcoal lighter. I saved the chukar cape for flytying purposes, poured a lot of bourbon over a little ice in a big tin cup, and sat down on a flat rock.

I wasn't too sure how far we'd come, but I knew we were somewhere south of the Crow Indian Reservation, in the Pryor Mountains of the Custer National Forest. The original Crow Reservation was formed in 1851 by federal fiat and covered 38 million acres of present-day Montana and Wyoming. Today, for a variety of reasons, the tribe's holdings have shrunk to a little over two million acres. There are 4,500 Crow living here with 1,000 at Crow Agency, the Reservation's largest town. Coal, oil, and natural gas along with some tourist money fuel the sparse economy.

The country both on and surrounding the reservation is fantastic, surreal country slipping off quietly into timelessness. Viewed from Interstate 90 running along the eastern edge, you see wave after wave of serrated hills, tree-lined creek bottoms, some Ponderosa pine stands, and miles of grass and sage. The mountains are more like uplifted badlands with the exception of two blocks of ridges that culminate in 8,822-foot East Pryor Mountain. I could see new snow, a lot, from a recent storm that blew swiftly away across northern Wyoming and South Dakota last week.

I learned from a geology textbook (some use anyway) I carried in the Toyota that the rocks we'd been scrambling around on were Paleozoic sedimentary formations, mainly limestone except where running water had sliced down to older rock. The entire range was a large chunk of basement and younger sedimentary rocks that were pushed east about 50 million years back. Not far from where I was reading and delicately sipping my drink, there are several large ice caves, caves that open vertically so only colder, denser air can enter them, bringing moisture that stays frozen year round, insulated by the porous limestone.

Dinosaur remains were discovered here in the 1960s. They were small, for dinosaurs, like large ostriches and ran on two feet. Apparently they were meateaters because the middle toenail on each foot was basically a wicked knife designed for slashing intended food sources. Paleontologists think that based on these findings, this species must have been quick (it had to run down prey) and agile (it had to stand on one foot while carving up its intended dinner). Until punt guns are once again legal, I'll stick with the chukars.

I could see West Pryor Mountain, 6,690 feet, northwest of me on the reservation. Looking at my maps earlier, I noticed several creeks were indicated. Trout? Catfish? Not likely. They were dry, bone dry. The muddy reaches were cracked wide open into large irregular shapes. The edges curled up. Where there had been at least the illusion of current earlier in the year, the streambeds were now just bleached rock and gravel. There was water, a lot of it, to the east in the Bighorn Canyon and the Bighorn River below Afterbay Dam (but this was the seventies and the Crow had the water closed to all non-tribal members and legal battles were still being fought over access. The fishing was probably hell on wheels. It's not bad right now in the nineties, either).

I seared the bird after rubbing it with a mixture of olive oil, garlic, and black pepper. I sautéed some mushroom caps filled with small chunks of feta cheese in white wine and butter, completing the feast. The hound got a few to keep him quiet. It was now dark and getting cold. I built the fire back up and sipped the bourbon neat, chain-smoking Camel straights. The high life as usual.

There were no lights out here and the stars dropped right down to the ground, glowing behind the pockets of grass and sage and winking behind the bluffs and mountains. Meteors sizzled across the sky.

College. Give me a break. I decided right then to work hard at staying in this country and probably remain reasonably broke in the process. (This has proved out with some accuracy. I'm still in Montana and I don't have a lot of money. Good family, though.)

Earlier, just as the sun went under, I saw some birds circling around the rocks we'd worked earlier. They were aiming for where the chukar had flushed. Out of sight we heard a bunch of abrupt *chucks* and higher pitched sounds. Nesting and homing calls? Bonzo looked in their direction without raising his head. Tomorrow we'd hunt 'em up again.

Ah-oooo. Ah-oooo.
"What the hell?," I mumbled sitting up in the sleeping bag.
Ah-oooo.
The damn dog was sitting on his haunches howling at the rising sun. Or at least the thought of it. The sky above was purple with stars and a slice of leftover moon. Lighter blue shading to the vaguest suggestion of pink was the extent of the action along the eastern front. I had to admit it was nearly six and I did go to sleep around midnight. Bonzo was famous (try renting in a college town with a wolfhound) for his early morning sessions. I covered the evenings. He took care of the days.

It only took a week to get dressed, rebuild the fire, and start some coffee in an old porcelain-coated pot. You know the type. I poured off a large mug full with plenty of grounds. After killing off the contents of the pot, I felt much better. Bonzo had polished off another five pounds of chicken necks. We were down to our last forty (at five cents a pound, they were cheaper than Gainesburgers), or five days' worth if we stretched things and I managed to hit a few chukars each day.

Back in the rocks that morning, the hound jumped the birds and I was ready and hit one that plowed into a rock wall and swung on another that crashed into the sage below. My first double in Montana on anything other than fool hens (spruce grouse).

College? What's that? I could do this forever, and the next few days seemed like heaven, but I knew I had to get back to Missoula and face the music. I had to either quit or change my attitude. I knew I'd quit. My faculty advisor was a dim image that I saw only at the East Gate Lounge when I went in for a quick one or to buy some package goods and the professor (one of the good ones) was bellied up with some of his literary cohorts. Or maybe he'd bum a smoke off me in the hall on campus, which didn't happen often because I was never there.

I stopped in at the cafe in Bridger and showed the boys and the waitress one of the chukars I was bringing home.

"So that's what they look like," and they were laughing like crazy again.

"See you next fall," and I was on my way back to Missoula.

That was my first chukar hunt and one of the best during a strange (stranger?) time in my life. I did quit school and I have no idea what my last quarter's grades were. Nor do I care. That's all ancient history like the ostrich dinosaurs lying stone-cold dead, embedded in very old rock.

Chukars are not all that common in Montana or the rest of the West for that matter, though once found, they are often present in good numbers. Supposedly there are some in the open country in and around the Flathead Indian Reservation south of Flathead Lake in the western third of the state. I've never seen any when I've been down there chasing largemouth bass and northern pike, and I have only heard the weakest of rumors regarding the birds' possible presence. Reportedly, there are chukars an hour or

so east of Great Falls, but I've never ground-truthed the verity of that information either.

They may be holding out in other isolated pockets of vertiginous rock and cactus flats in some lonesome outpost. Those are birds that are discovered by accident while doing something else, like chasing rumors of large coveys of sharptails or running down some bizarre report of huge rainbows swimming in an un-fished spring creek burbling away out in the unlimited weirdness of the Missouri Breaks or points even farther into the obscure. You never know what will turn up on the road.

Over the years there have not been many chukars in my bag, but when I have found them, it's usually been before noon or near sunset on relatively open ground hanging against steep, rocky slopes. There has always been sage and cactus. They like to roost near the ridgetops, but will move down to water around mid-morning early in the season during dry years. After tanking up, they tend to disperse to feed or screw around during the main part of the day.

When I've come across the birds lower down, they nearly always fly straight to the top of the roughest country in the area after the initial shooting. If more birds are in the program, plan on a tough climb toward the crest or just over the edge. They won't be anywhere else. The birds do seem to hold prior to the first flush, in fact much better than Western pheasants.

Other hunters have relayed tales of dozens of chukars bunched up after the snow flies, and this is no doubt true. I've never been in the country in November; six hundred miles of driving down from my home in Whitefish through wind, slush, ice, and blinding snow are props for an extended nightmare. Chukars will also be holding down lower after it snows, or so I'm told. Glassing the ridges can help locate the birds as they move across the skyline or begin to head downhill.

Noting where the birds land, if for some reason they do not crest the ridge, often proves productive. Working sidehill, a tough proposition frequently entailing climbing up, over, or more likely around rock outcroppings, turns up chukars that seem to hold at the same elevation much the way subsurface feeding trout do in a river or lake. They are all at the same level. Two hunters, one lower than the perceived bird level, working horizontally, can have excellent shooting. The upper person basically forces the chukars to fly down past the lower shooter. A well-trained, close-working dog serves the same purpose.

A 20-gauge or light 12 double barrel is my preference for this type of work for a couple of reasons: The less weight I have to lug up and downhill, the better, and the lighter guns are easier to mount and swing in rough terrain often pitched at severe angles. No. 7½ shot seems adequate, though 6s are not out of line in tighter quarters. Full and modified chokes have proved out in chukar country.

According to Charlie Waterman in his excellent 1972 book *Hunting Upland Birds*, records indicate that chukars were introduced into this country from the furnace-hot deserts of India as early as 1893. Red-legged partridges from Spain and Holland to Inner Mongolia have also been used with limited success. From 1932 to the time of that book's writing, perhaps as many as one million birds were released.

The early fifties saw the"boom"in chukar shooting that now ranges over parts of Arizona, California, Colorado, Idaho, Montana, Nevada, Oregon, Utah, Wyoming, British Columbia, Hawaii, and possibly even Baja California and New Zealand. The birds have been as high as 12,000 feet in the White Mountains of California, and below sea level in Death Valley (not surprisingly, I've found myself at this negative elevation on occasion, drinking Buckhorn beer, usually not far from Zabriski Point. We all have our weaknesses).

Extreme heat and cold are not crucial factors in the birds' survival, but heavy snow is. They head quickly to lower elevations when winter storms move in. Rain tends to scatter the chukars, though they also tend to regroup faster than other upland species, making a high-pitched racket doing so. The birds make a variety of sounds and calls, but their language is unintelligible to me. They will often be found feeding in cheatgrass which, in turn, is found along with sage. Chicks rely heavily on insects. Predators include the usual list of suspects: hawks, owls, eagles, coyotes, bobcats, foxes, and snakes.

Waterman recounts some intriguing stories about the life of a chukar in Asia. Tribesman riding ponies kill the birds with long whips (perhaps this is where magazine editors go to school). And some Asiatic chukars are domesticated and kept as fighting cocks.

Chukars are certainly an exotic in all senses of the word. They hang out in remote, inhospitable country, are uniquely marked, originate in some of the wildest country in Asia, and are bearers of a harsh heritage. As Thomas McIntyre said in *The Way of the Hunter*:

> If the walking is the point, then the most heroic walking in upland-bird hunting is in the pursuit of chukar...How to describe a day of it: taking the stairs in the Empire State Building, street level to observation deck, over and over, the stairwell either too warm or much too cold, the air thin as Tibet's, with the Muzak on the fritz, nearly captures it.

More than"nearly."

G uide or no guide, dog or no dog, I headed out to the Pryors in early October after an absence of several years. Still, that country could not have changed much at all. I was alone this time, without Bonzo, who'd passed on many years ago. Instead of the Landcruiser, I was driving an old Toyota pickup (still more foreign silliness). Shotguns, food and beverages, camping gear, a few fly-rods, and a bunch of split larch for the fire filled the rig, both in the cab and in back.

The drive was about twelve hours over several mountain passes through Butte, Bozeman, and finally down the highway into Bridger where I stopped for fries and a cheeseburger. There was a new crew here — the next generation of ranchers and town residents — but they were just as friendly, offering essentially the same advice as I'd received in the seventies. Tired, I drove a gravel road that wound around hills and along a small creek bottom to a small, deserted campground just below a fish hatchery. The evening was clear and the long-range forecast called for warm, dry weather during the next week. A strong high pressure system was parked overhead, holding the nastiness of the approaching winter at bay above the Canadian border.

I saw some sharptails on the way in, so I grabbed the Beretta and walked over a low hill above the little creek. I started working up a narrow, brushy draw, kicking through the undergrowth in hopes of finding some grouse. I realized that as soon as our aging Australian shepherd passed away (I hope not any time soon), I'd get a dog I could train (to some extent) like a springer or perhaps another golden retriever. I needed a bird dog and a road companion. The golden back at home was a great dog and my buddy, but he'd devoted himself to protecting my family and chasing tennis balls. His life was full.

Near the narrowing top of the chute, four sharptails flew up with loud, fast-beating wings, and I rolled one into the side of the grassy hill. Too burned out from the driving, I picked the grouse up and walked back to camp for a quick dinner of ham-and-cheese sandwiches. Then it was time to nod off.

The next morning was clear, the sun just coming up. Hot coffee and a bagel, and then I saw the brown trout rising steadily to small caddis that were whirring all over the water. I couldn't resist casting to a few. They were bright golden fish with black and red spotting and dark brown backs — fish to fourteen inches — and I knew that this was a sign that I was home free. The chukars would be where they always were. Packing quickly, I charged down the road, happy and keeping time to Little Village on the cassette.

Rising up onto the plateau, I was spotted by a herd of antelope that raced alongside for a brief distance before bounding off across the flat and swiftly out of sight. Small heads atop stretched-out necks watched me from a field of sage before turning tail and ducking from view. Sage grouse. I marked them for when I came out.

Pulling off the road and bumping over the uneven ground, I pulled into the site of my first camp in this part of the world. I'd been here a few times over the years and each time, the place looked unchanged. No sign of recent fires, no beer cans or other litter, no footprints. Nothing. Exactly the way I'd left it the last time, each time.

I grabbed the shotgun, packed a small bottle of water and a candy bar, and marched off to the rocky hills. The sagebrush was taller than I remembered and the cactus was plentiful. The spiny plants were brown-green, a little shrunken from the heat and dryness of last summer. At the base of the rocks, I paused to eat the candy and drink some water.

"Hi-ho, onward and upward, hoopy-toopy ten-four," I said aloud, knowing that order was beginning to break down already. The climb up seemed so much harder than twenty years ago. I stopped often to catch my wind. Only a T-shirt and light cotton shirt, yet I was perspiring. Temperature nearing seventy, I guessed.

Looking back across the sage flat, the truck appeared small, matchbox-like from this distance and altitude. Objects were already shimmering in the mounting warmth down below.

Where Bonzo had turned the chukars that first time was only a few yards up ahead, past a sheet of broken rock. On top of this was the level spit of grass and bush. Breathing hard again, I looked around. The crest was a hundred feet above, so I walked right through all of the cover and around the piles of rock. Nothing.

Maybe farther up. Finally to the ridge, the view was fantastic. The Beartooths in the southwest were covered in white. The convoluted high plains, cut in meandering slices by creeks and small rivers, stretched off in all directions. The breeze up here was cool, fresh with the hint of sage and the distant snowfields. Time passed. Who cared. This was serene. I lay down and napped. No hurry. There was time.

Sometimes I'm not sure why I wake up, what triggers the hazy rise up through sweet oblivion into consciousness. I think I dreamed of the two weeks in April I'd spent fishing, wandering, camping, and cruising with a friend from Vermont who was out here researching a novel on buffalo hunters from another century. As I was not really awake, things seemed surreal, too bright and sharp, glowing around the edges.

The slightest of sounds. Again. There! Again. Strange conversation barely heard. The chukars. They were down below, feeding in the cheatgrass. There they were — a dozen, maybe more. If I moved, they'd see me and fly all the way down the slope opposite camp.

They disappeared around a confusion of cracked rock, so I rolled back over the other side and sidehilled it as quickly as I could to move well ahead of what I guessed their course would be. After a half-mile, there was a slight cut in the ridge. I crept through it and worked slowly down to where I thought the birds would show. And I waited, for long, long minutes. Had they passed or spooked? The wind seemed right, quartering uphill and toward the northeast, away from the covey. Still they didn't show. I'd blown it.

A hint of movement, and there they were — almost even with me on the slope, moving without a care, pausing here and there to snag some fallen seed or a bit of grit. They moved steadily. I slipped the safety off. The gun came up as I stood, and the birds broke wildly, down and away. I picked up one nearest me, swinging through and below while firing, and the bird bounced downhill trailing feathers. Another, a late flyer, was only feet off the ground, still climbing, and he was an easy shot, like jump-shooting ducks coming out of thick cattails along an ice-choked stream.

I watched as the others flew far away down from me, screaming close to the ground and breaking tightly out of view around a curve in the hill.

My hands were shaking so badly, I had trouble picking up the dead chukars, having to remember to use the free hand and not the one holding the gun in a death grip. What a rush. I should be doing this every day of the season. Screw the writing and the fall-run browns and all the rest of it. This was *everything*.

Carefully setting the Beretta in a clump of grass, I held the birds, one in each hand. The red legs were a shade less intense than the beaks. The blacks of the masks and throat were like obsidian, shining in the light. The grays of the chest and shoulders were like the hard granite of the peaks of Glacier Park.

I'd planned to try to shoot my limit each day of the trip, but these two were plenty. I'd walk back to camp and take my time preparing a fine dinner before fading out beneath the stars and a sliver of new moon.

The lowlands and distant mountains and streams shimmered in the October light that was at once brilliant and subdued.

I wish Bonzo was here. He appreciated these things.

Chapter Four

Ruffed Grouse

The grouse have always been here, ever since I first started hunting this triangular piece of forested land. There are spruce grouse holding deep in the dark thickness of cedar and fir that grow densely alongside the creeks and seeps. And higher up, near 6,000 feet, there are blues holding tight to the breezy ridges.

More importantly to me, there are ruffed grouse, plenty of them, wandering among the pines that rise up in sharp relief next to the large clearcuts that are only now, after twenty years or more, beginning to come back. Larch and pine, bright green in their youth, are filling in the scars of excessive logging that is the hideous heritage of unchecked cutting on the Tally Lake Ranger District of the Flathead National Forest in northwest Montana.

I first found this country in the early eighties while tracking down a small lake purported to hold fat grayling, silvery salmonids distinguished by sail-like dorsal fins studded with turquoise and iridescent purples and dark spots. The fish were present, and on that first outing, easy to catch on small dry flies.

Driving home, I turned up an old logging road that twisted around the southern edge of the triangle, coursing through clearcuts that barely showed signs of revegetation — small pines of a foot or so tall fighting to stretch above the downed slash and tight growth of fireweed, an ugly plant except when in lavender bloom. Coming around a sharp bend, I was surprised by the sight of a group of ruffed grouse taking on loads of grit on the edge of the rocky road. I stopped the truck, unsheathed the shotgun, slowly opened the door, and stepped out. The birds looked up and then went back to work. I was tempted to blast a couple off the ground, but didn't (not really tempted, but seeing grouse acting like such morons always prompts the notion). Instead I walked up to them, to within ten feet. The grouse were oblivious. The appelation "fool hen" for mountain grouse seemed apt.

One finally spooked and lifted off and I shot it. The bird fell back to the road just beyond the others, who stopped pecking at the ground and walked over to their downed comrade, making nervous little *clicks* as they approached. Then they went back to gathering grit for their gizzards. I replaced the spent shell and took a few steps closer. Three more went up, straight up with quick beats of their wings, and two more collapsed to the ground in a tiny blizzard of brown feathers. The rest walked over to these two, examined the situation with a few more *clucks*, and went back to their business.

This was ridiculous. Three of their number were dead only inches away, and they were more intent on the grit. The limit was four and I filled this out with two more steps and two more shots that hit one as the birds finally broke for the woods. Some latent survival instinct had finally kicked in. Certainly not the most challenging shooting around, but ruffs are superb table fare and they *were* in the air when I shot them.

A couple days later I pulled over to the same spot. Almost thankfully there were no grouse standing in the road. I dropped off from the road. The walk through the fireweed, negotiating the downed logs and hidden stump, was a bitch, especially working uphill to the timber covering the hills above. Armed with both a camera and a gun, I stepped out of the bright, airy spaces of the clearcut and into the trees. A different world. One of silence and subdued, green-shaded, light.

Twenty feet and the surroundings changed from the real to the mysterious, the dark. Elk and deer pellets were everywhere in small shiny brown piles. "Milk Duds" zipped through my mind. Pretty sad there, Holt. Bowl-shaped depressions in the decaying, red-brown powder of long-fallen pines indicated that the ruffed grouse used the area for dusting, and probably loafing and feeding. Farther on, a number of lodgepole pines bore scratch marks. The laid-bare, yellow-white outer wood oozed sticky, amber sap. The recent work of a black bear (grizzlies were an exceptional rarity on this part of the forest in northwest Montana. They held out far back in the rugged peaks and isolated drainages a few air miles east of here in the Whitefish Range, the Bob Marshall Wilderness, and in Glacier Park). The black had stretched tight leg and back muscles and filed sharp claws even sharper. The marks rose a foot or more above my head. A big animal. Oh well. I wasn't afraid of bears. I respected them, but I wasn't scared. They and their big cousins, the grizzlies, made this part of the world special, alive. Without the bears, the forest would have a dull, juiceless character in my eyes. Not as bad as the trashiness of a Disney World horror show, more like the Wind Rivers in Wyoming. Spectacular, special country, but lacking something, like an animal that could knock you into the next time zone if his mood was right.

Working deeper into the forest and still uphill through thick patches of huckleberry too late in the season for the sweet, dark-blue fruit, I saw a small, grassy opening just ahead where light shone against the dark of the pines. The grass was dull tan with some shafts of fading green, reminders of a summer that ran off too quickly for my taste. Small dark shapes were moving around in the tiny meadow. The *grouse*. I dropped down on hands and knees and inched closer, the camera hanging from my neck snagging on limbs and brush the entire way, jerking my head down. On the edge of the clearing, I sat cross-legged and shot two rolls of black-and-white film using an 80-210mm lens. The birds were aware of my presence. Some even moved closer, filling the lens, in order to gain a better view of the large intruder. (The shots turned out and I've sold them time and again to newspapers and outdoor magazines. *Easy money*.)

I felt guilty about the thought of killing any of these grouse. So guilty, that I shed the camera, stood up and shot two as they took off away from me into the dimness of the pines.

After working so hard for the birds in northern Wisconsin and the Upper Peninsula of Michigan, and after hearing and reading so much about the mystique and difficult shooting ruffed grouse present, I thought, "Bullshit. These guys are simple." I would soon learn a different tune, one not easily played.

The upland season was young and the birds in this pocket of the forest had not yet been hunted. As the weeks advanced and I worked deeper into this country hunting different populations in ever harsher, thicker terrain, I learned that the birds fly like demons, sliding and twisting through tangled branches and bend ing around tree trunks. Frustrated, I would often climb even higher searching for blues or work my way down swampy draws of sweet-smelling cedar looking for world-class-dumb spruce grouse. The blues were better flyers, screaming out of range over the ridges. The spruce would fly into the limbs (ruffs do this at times). I'd throw a stick to make them fly, trying to guess which way they'd break. Wrong half the time, I always got entertaining shooting, trying to throw then bring the gun to bear and instantly track the grouse, who by now knew they'd best beat cheeks if living another day was of any moment.

The ruffed grouse knew what they were doing, that much was obvious; the first two outings were flukes, and I'm glad this was so. Popping the birds with such ease would have turned stultifying in a hurry. The more recent efforts had proved far better sport. Hitting grouse on these outings required swift reactions and long leads (and some luck). Dropping one of the birds now made me feel like an accomplished shot, one of the seasoned veterans, even though I knew better.

Now, some ten years after that first fall, I know where the covers and the birds are, at least within certain parameters. Slipping along the side of that meadow, I jumped a bunch in front of me that were quickly gone before the echoes of my shooting had died. Gunsmoke rose slowly in the lifeless air, blending with the scent of pine that was strong and fresh from a light rain last night. I'd bring a dog next time. My goofy golden retriever, the one who loves pursuing tennis balls. He'd get a kick out of this silliness. Birds, gunfire, and Master swearing at the trees. High adventure for Zachary.

I walked on, putting up two singles and a pair. They all flew easily to safety amid a hail of errant 7 ½'s and a delicate shower of pine needles. Obviously, this hunt was one of those tweedy, plus-fours occasions. Let's spread a checkered tablecloth on the ground, open a vintage bottle of some delicate white of exotic lineage, and eat ridiculous little sandwiches that don't have crusts. Maybe watercress and a thin spread of mayonnaise, or how about some Canada goose *foie gras*? You bet. Give me a shot of Jack and a strong cigar. No ruffs today, but at least I'd leave a calling card reeking of Honduran tobacco and bonded whiskey. The grouse would know that an individual of taste and refinement had passed their way, and none too quietly either. Class will always tell.

> That all who know the grouse come to have an affection for this unpredictable thunderbolt of the uplands, is axiomatic. Its rolling drum and roaring flush add a personality to the woods which nothing can replace. Its uncanny skill in foiling the sportsman has endeared it to all who prize a worthy opponent.

So said Gardiner Bump in his preface to *The Ruffed Grouse* in the spring of 1942. The book, published by the New York state conservation department five decades ago, contains more information than I'll ever be able to assimilate concerning the species. Still, it was one of the first titles I read that revealed the reverence, fascination, and even awe that hunters held for the birds.

When I first started hunting ruffed grouse and woodcock in the North Woods of the Midwest, I had little interest in the lore, history, or science of the sport. I was interested in finding and hitting the birds. This was great country filled with whitetail, lynx, muskies, brook trout, walleyes, eagles, and osprey. I spent a lot of time hunting and fishing up there, catching big musky, little brookies, and shooting a lot of ruffed grouse and a few woodcock. The time seems all that much better today as I look back to hours running into weeks that held no worry or dread of bills, family responsibilities, or entanglements with my typewriter.

As time passed, I learned through much walking in the forest where the grouse might be found in autumn. Experiencing any success with shooting, especially when the poplars and birch were still full of leaves, was another matter. But as the trees dropped their leaves, carpeting the ground in a lofty pile of brown, tan, and gray, the country opened up and I started to shoot a little better. As the seasons accumulated, like the fallen leaves, I probably reached my apogee of successful shooting, resulting in one bird for every four shots when working country I knew well.

I can still smell the damp leaves of late October, and I'll never forget the cold shock, when splashing through small brooks, of water that slipped between minute openings in my old boots. Or the grouse hurtling up out of nowhere in front of my friend's flushing dog. Our quick yelps of surprise at the outburst, hearts pounding, all senses instantly keyed on the birds. The shooting. And less often, watching the dog retrieve the ruffed grouse, the bird hanging limply from the dog's jaws.

Bump got it right in that one paragraph, and he locked in with this from the same book:

> *Whatever contributes to make our life more attractive usually finds a place in history. So it is that, furnishing both food and sport, the ruffed grouse has reserved for itself a fascinating niche in man's annals of the past. The larger part of the story is, of course, tucked away in memories, but an astonishing amount has been permanently preserved in written form.*

A quick scan of my library reveals that I own more titles about ruffed grouse than any other bird. Titles like: *Bare November Days, Ruffed Grouse, Drummer in the Woods, An Affair with Grouse, Upland Passage,* and so on.

There is something about this elusive bird that draws writers, not to mention hunters, unchecked into a pursuit that, in its most benign manifestations, borders on addiction. There are the givens such as wonderful country, well-trained dogs, the time spent with old (and new-found) friends — there is all of this and something more. Perhaps the fact that we have been hunting the grouse for centuries back East in places like upstate New York and Vermont has some bearing on the matter. Maybe because of this, the grouse really has reserved a niche in the annals of the past.

I remember visiting my friend Bob Jones and his wife Louise at their home in the mountains of Vermont early one December. We went hunting only one afternoon during my stay. We had all the right excuses for such behavior, for only doing this once. We hadn't seen each other in some time, and there was whiskey to drink and stories to tell. And there were Louise's superb meals. Didn't want to risk missing those. All enjoyable, worthwhile, and necessary, but I still remember that one outing. If one shot can define a season, so can one day walking the woods define upland bird hunting.

We drove up a steep hill in Bob's rig with his yellow Lab, Jake, and his Jack Russell, Ros (hell, if I can hunt chukar with an Irish wolfhound, Bob can damn well hunt with any breed he chooses). The day was cold, in the low twenties, with high clouds that allowed a weak sun to cast a filtered, golden glow over the countryside.

The dogs were eager, dragging us along with their enthusiasm, and we worked quickly up into some thick cover that offered not only the promise of grouse, but thorns as well. We worked that piece hard, the dogs pounded back and forth, close in, Jake's bell tinkling like hard cider. Ros zipped along with an intensity and sense of purpose that showed that she knew what this game was all about. Moving to another cover not far away, we wheeled around its perimeter covering a lot of ground. Bob kindly let me handle the outside edge; as he confidently worked to my right, I frantically quick-marched to keep up. Home-field advantage. The ground was frozen hard except where small springs perked through the ground. You found these by stepping through the snow and down into a gray mush. Cold-water memories brought to life.

We pushed up and down for several hours without seeing a ruff. There were plenty of tracks, and there were thrashed-out clearings in the snow and branches rubbed raw that indicated rutting deer. The lack of birds was not important. To be out in new country hunting with a friend when normally I'd be back home worrying about how to make it through the winter ("Hey, Lynda. Do you think *People Magazine* would be interested in a story on bull trout?") was a joy. Back at the truck, the dogs were a touch more sedate, only slightly worn from the excursion. They circled happily around our feet. We stowed the guns and I followed Bob to a small knoll that gave way to a view of his valley.

Far away, the small creek that dropped down out of the mountains behind his home wandered beneath dark-trunked trees, leafless, bare, waiting for the real winter to come. The clouds had cleared off the fields and the setting sun cast purple shadows on the white ground and the stubble poking through the snow. The distant ridges were edged in the softest of reds. No breeze. Not a whisper. No sound. Dead silence.

Time passed, then Bob caught my eye and smiled some and said,"Let's head back."

That was all and that was everything. You don't need to shoot the birds to understand, to feel the pull they exert, to have a fine time. There's so much more involved in it.

(The next spring, after spending some time with me in southeastern Montana, Bob returned home to Vermont only to blow a tire avoiding a grouse on the road. He T-boned a telephone pole, cut his face to some bloody extent, and worried all of us half to death. But he survived and terrorized the local population with, what I'm told, was a hideous visage. I bet he was smiling all through this. Later he told me he'd shot the grouse that caused the crash; he laughed and said,"It's fun to think so, anyway."And one more tale is added to the ruffed grouse library.)

I'm positive that all of this is responsible for much of the grouse's tight hold over so many of us, but there's more — it is the birds themselves.

The ruffed grouse of the Rocky Mountains differ in color from those of both the East and the Pacific woodlands. They are generally gray over the body and the tail, which does display the trademark dark band. Birds from other areas outside the northern Rockies also have a red-brown or rufous phase. The females are marginally duller in color, but basically indistinguishable from the males. Unless you see a bird drumming on a hollow log (a male) or sitting on a nest of six to fifteen eggs (a female), telling the two apart to many folks is borderline impossible. Males tend to run a bit larger than hens, anywhere from sixteen to nineteen inches. Also, the barring is less distinct on males. On cocks, ruffs are more obvious and tail feathers longer, but try determining this when the birds break madly from cover. I can't.

The same holds true regarding age determination once the grouse have lost their youthful fluff and grown post-juvenile plumage. Again, size is of some help, but by mid-season, irrelevant.

When spring finally hits the northern mountains, the sound of the drumming males is as sure a signal of the coming warmth and greening of the countryside as are the sounds of water running from melting snow. The first faint wingbeats are perceived almost subliminally. Hearing the distinctive sound is cause for celebration. Put the top down on the Buick Riveria, mix up a hearty batch of gin-and-tonics (don't forget the lime), and turn up the radio. It's hard to believe we've survived another winter.

A huge log, a remnant of the ancient forest that used to dominate these mountains, lies next to the guest cabin that serves as my office. From that log, the hollow boomings of a ruffed grouse filtered through the building's walls as I was writing away one morning in late March. Faint at first, then louder as both the intensity and my awareness of it increased. The article on pass-shooting for grasshoppers along the Missouri Breaks or whatever could wait.

Stepping lightly from my comfortable cell, I crept to the edge of the woods with a pair of binoculars and there was the bird, standing erect on the log, tail feathers stretched behind in support, wings flapping furiously for brief seconds, then relaxing. A glorious sight. What natural madness, this wild bird puffed up with assumed regality looking for a woman. It had to be spring.

I've watched the birds mount this particular log over the years, and grouse always spend large chunks of time finding just the right place to begin their concert. Each grouse selects the same spot on the log, near the higher, wider end. Better acoustics, no doubt. In the fall when they're not drumming away, they pick rose-hips and snowberries from bushes just outside my windows. The grouse stand on their toes, necks stretched, and pluck the fruit with furious little tugs. I've put off writing for an hour or more watching this marvelous exhibition.

I write this in the depths of a below-zero whiteout that has poured over the mountains to the west after roaring down from the Arctic, raising hell all the way, and now is pummeling my valley with frightful gusts of wind, I dream of sitting on the veranda of a cabana in some place warm, tropical, like Belize. The faithful houseboy and trusted fishing companion, Raul, has just delivered another round of strong, fruity rum drinks. Lynda and I talk casual-ly of little, if anything, maybe attending the bullfights in Spain in a week or so. Our children are being tutored by a qualified nanny

somewhere close at hand but out of sight and hearing (remember, this is a fantasy). My agent has just closed a screenplay deal to be based on my latest best-selling novel. The money is well in six figures. The Caribbean is calm and tranquil today. Maybe I'll head out to the flats and cast to bonefish.

Then the first warm zephyrs of spring float through the mountains, and I realize that part of the glory of this first taste of renewed life is the fact that another mean, cold season has been endured, weathered with at least a measure of dignity, style, and to some extent, sobriety. If the weather is always balmy, what is there to compare anything to? I like winter for this reason and a few others. The drumming of the grouse, like the first casts to rising trout, are part of this metamorphosis. The seasonal flow makes the Rockies special, charged with subtle shifts in intensity — a very jazz-like rhythm.

While spring seems to be prime drumming time, I've heard the grouse at all months of the year except January and February. Autumn seems to be a period of increased action by mature birds serving to define territory to warn off the yearlings. In the spring, this display is clearly intended to attract hens and may also serve to release excess energy, a lot like my golden rushing madly about the yard in blind circles after being cooped up inside all winter.

When I'm cooped up inside, I read a lot. Anything. Bad novels. Cereal boxes. The Radio Shack catalogue. Last winter, I spent time with a number of books on bird hunting and related subjects, tripping across some arcane information in the process. As an example of how intensely these birds have been studied, look at *Ruffed Grouse* (the one published by Stackpole). The authors cite studies conducted in Ontario and West Virginia that indicate the length of the drum ranges from 9.06 to 10.62 seconds, and that the average number of wingbeats per drum ranges from 45.5 to 49. The book is filled with these things. Amazing facts that are useful to me only from the perspective of curiosity.

Another interesting item gleaned from the book is the speculation that certain dominant males "stimulate other males to occupy drumming sites nearby." Apparently, aggressive young males move into position to challenge older birds, drawn, in fact, by the elders' drumming. Competition wherever you look.

One spring evening, I watched a proud bird drumming away on the log, only to see this huge, gray blur swoop down through the pines, legs slanting forward, talons extended. A great gray owl with a wingspan of five feet just missed a gourmet dinner through the slightest of miscalculations, dusting the grouse in a minor stir of displaced feathers. The attack knocked the ruff over and it dropped from view, but I heard it drumming away the next day. Sexual drives will be the death of all of us, and this drumming must serve as a tantalizing magnet to avian predators far and wide. Hearing the telltale sound, hawks and owls must take to the air with atavistic bloodlust. Attracting a mate is dangerous business. I'm reminded of my carousing nights in the bars of Beloit, Wisconsin. Bloodied noses and bruised hands. Intense times.

In the early days back in Wisconsin, I found the grouse by asking a lot of questions, tracking down suspect leads, and plain, blind stumbling into the birds while tramping through the woods or some malarial bog in search of world-record brook trout (that seldom exceeded six inches), or while verifying rumors (they were true only one time) of huge muskies spawning in small, woodland streams. The grouse always turned up in dense forest that was also moist, often riddled with skinny creeks and anemic seeps. And they always seemed to be around the unkempt apple orchards that the locals cultivated with a sort of zealous pride at the outset, but gradually allowed to fall into neglect as their enthusiasm diminished over the decades. Personally, I think the ruffs got a buzz off the apples lying on the ground that had begun to ferment. Some of the flushes I remember were anything but swift or adroit. Clumsy was more like it, the birds clipping limbs and flying erratically at my approach.

In Montana the location process was similar, though much easier. There seemed to be more birds and they were not hunted with anything resembling vehemence. Not many people pursue grouse with any enthusiasm in the western third of the state. Big game is king, along with pheasants in the valley fields. But enough people knew about the birds to point me in some right directions, and I normally followed up on any sign I spotted while out tromping about or when I actually saw the grouse as I drove the logging roads in search of that one fantastic, undiscovered trout stream or lake or bog. Within a few years, I had accumulated a number of covers around the region, all reasonably dependable when the ebb and flow of population cycles was factored into the equation.

The elevation was higher and the country more severe than its North Woods counterpart, but there were many similarities: thick forest running up against large openings, often clearcuts or secondary growth, and water. If the area had plenty of food and good cover but scant water, the grouse were not present. Marshy spots, small springs, creeks — that was all it took, provided they were in good cover, protected from predators, especially those circling above.

Regarding diet, the ruffed grouse, considering its habitat, is catholic in its tastes. The crops of many grouse I've cleaned have contained an assortment of leaves, buds (especially from aspen trees and brushy willows), and berries including huckleberries, serviceberries, and even rosehips. I've also turned up crickets, grasshoppers, pine needles, and pine nuts.

Regarding aspen trees, studies have proven that they are a major food source. They also provide superb cover. Where I've found scattered copses or, better yet, large, uncrowded stands of aspen that also contain adequate ground cover, I've also found my best covers.

One spot not far from home is ideal habitat with a few acres of aspen plopped in the middle. The trees are all growing discrete distances from each other, maybe eight to ten feet. The ground cover is brushy, tangled, and crisscrossed with game paths and small clearings of grass. Every time I come here, I put up birds. Early in the year when the leaves are golden, the setting is calender-perfect but difficult shooting. The grouse leap into the air and vanish. I've consistently limited out on downed leaves, limbs, and twigs. Later, when the leaves are off, the birds are still around and much easier to shoot, "easier" being a relative term. At least I get a second or two more to track their flight paths. I've never seen another bird hunter at this place, which further convinces me that grouse hunting is no big deal in my country.

After the first cat's-paw snow, finding the grouse is simplified. I follow their tracks and often turn up birds. If the increasing frequency of their droppings is any indication, the grouse are aware of my presence, perhaps a touch rattled. As the snow accumulates, my hunting fever subsides. After several feet have piled up, I rarely see the grouse. They do have a toe protrusion or snowshoe that allows them to track in fluffy powder with some degree of mobility. And most intriguing to me, when the snow reaches a foot or more in depth, the birds instinctively burrow in the powder (the Eurasian black grouse spends up to ninety-five percent of its time hiding this way from severe weather). Sometimes they actually dive into the snow, where they hollow out a small cave. Their body warmth softens the snow walls that then harden into secure shelter. Snow is an excellent insulator and the birds do quite well in these holes. I've never seen the birds hit the banks, but I've startled one that exploded out of a pile of the stuff, trailing a comet of snow, wings pounding as it fled to the aspens across the road. Some reports indicate that this survival technique is not without danger. Powder covering crusted snow or hiding rocks or logs can lead to broken necks when the ruffed grouse sail headfirst into the banks. Life is tough.

There have been times when I've put on snowshoes and pushed into covers near home looking for the birds. I found them in singles (I think) huddled in small spaces of hollow logs or holes in the snow cover. I can look right at them, the ambient light reflecting off their eyes. They never move. They seem unafraid, or perhaps it's just too damn cold out to bother with flight. A nice sight in the harsh, dead heart of an ugly January, the birds snuggly tucked away while storm clouds roll in from the northwest. Pine boughs are bent under heavy loads of snow. It's so cold you can sometimes hear trees splinter. Except for me and the birds and maybe Zachary plowing away somewhere nearby, nose buried, the world seems dead. The concept of spring is a cruel joke, a Chinese water torture of agonizingly long, brutally cold, dark days substituted for the dropping water. I wonder what the grouse feel.

The range of the ruffed grouse in Montana encompasses nearly all of the mountainous western third of the state along with isolated pockets in the center of the state. In other parts of the West they are found in the Black Hills of South Dakota, the northern mountains of Idaho, parts of Wyoming, and the coastal forests of the Pacific northwest as far south as northern California.

As for the perfect gun for ruffed grouse, opinion varies. I use my 20 because I'm comfortable with it, even though the full and modified chokes are less than ideal in close quarters when the birds blow up in my face.

In *New England Grouse Shooting,* William Harnden Foster says:"An ideal grouse gun may be defined broadly as the one that a certain hunter will find most pleasant to carry to the spot where a grouse is to be shot at, and there prove most efficient when the shot is made."

My friend and shotgunning authority Michael McIntosh says that a 28-gauge having one barrel open and the second"bored to true modified purely shines."And three-quarter ounces of No. 7 1/2 works as well as any load for me. Now if I can only scrape up the cash for a"Best"28-gauge.

Montana was showing off this October morning as I started to climb up and over timbered mountains.The narrow road cruised ever upward in a series of severe switchbacks. At a turnout on the edge of a sharp ravine I pulled over and lit a Camel. Looking back the way I'd come, I could see the Whitefish Range rising behind the town of Eureka, the nearly vertical flanks of the peaks shimmering shades of filtered blue in the light haze.The mountains guarding Fernie, British Columbia over the border looked like a fortress of sheer walls and jagged granite abutments. The cigarette tasted good. I said to myself I'd quit someday soon. Damn straight.

Forty miles to go before reaching a wild, unspoiled valley tucked beneath bare summits and pine-covered slopes. An isolated nook of sanity over near Idaho somewhere. A place of civilized decadence and freedom.The area's residents practiced the high art of enjoying life, raising a little hell, and working only as required with well-honed dispatch. A fine corner of the world.

I was bound for Tim Linehan's place, a small, comfortable cabin tucked back in the trees not far from the valley's beautiful, free-form river. I'd met the energetic guy at an Orvis Rendezvous for guides and outfitters held at Chico Hot Springs not far from the Yellowstone River in the Paradise Valley.This was a few years back, and he'd generously insisted that I come over and hunt ruffed grouse with him one autumn in the future. That time had arrived.

The day was warming quickly and I rode it with the windows of the truck rolled down. Spruce grouse were making casual appearances alongside the road here and there. One of the forks of the main river flowed easily beneath thick pines that gave way quickly and unfortunately to a series of large clearcuts. The Kootenai National Forest had an even worse management legacy than the Flathead. I once quoted a former forest supervisor in an article for *Fly Fisherman* magazine on the deleterious effects logging our national forests had on trout streams. The guy actually said, "Cutting the suitable timber base in Glacier National Park would be for the greater social good," and a member of the timber industry added that "Wilderness is like herpes. Once you get it, it's forever."

You had to marvel at this Dark Ages mentality, especially in light of the fact that less than ten percent of the old-growth forest is still standing in northwest Montana. Both of these gentle souls now write a blizzard of Letters to the Editor under the guise of concerned private citizens.

The valley I was now swiftly descending into had taken its share, more than its share, of hits in this regard, but the country was so damn good, so resilient, it was hanging on and even regenerating. This was prime land, as good as the state has to offer.

When I first stumbled upon the drainage in the early seventies, the streams held large brook, westslope, rainbow, bull, and very rare redband trout, along with large numbers of native mountain whitefish. All species are still present today, but in lesser numbers and smaller sizes. There have always been big mule and whitetail deer, elk, a few grizzlies, black bears, mountain lions, and lots of mountain grouse — spruce, blue, and ruffed. To some extent, the recovering clearcuts have provided increased habitat for the ruffed grouse, but even this fragile balance between habitat and overcutting appears to have been tipped to the negative side of things.

Perhaps with this country's belated shift in emphasis to preserving what's left and trying to rehabilitate what's been trashed, this part of the world and Montana in general will recover. Not in my lifetime, for sure, but maybe somewhere down the road.

By the time I reached the West Fork, only miles from Tim's place, it was noon, so I pulled over to walk along the river. A sandwich and a beer went well as I hopped from rock to rock upstream. Small caddis helicoptered above the dark water, aspen leaves whirled about in small eddies and slipped over a series of cascades. No fish, though. Moving into the trees, I spotted some fresh grouse droppings and thought I heard distant drumming. Probably wishful foreshadowing. Later, cruising through a very small town, I noticed that the local taverns had a few customers, pickups parked in front of the establishments were loaded with firewood, chain saws lying on top as were some dogs, stretched out in the warmth of the day.

Rolling into Tim's front yard, I found him cleaning out the back of his truck. Boxes of shotgun shells, assorted empties, sundry coolers, and a couple of shotguns were scattered about. Tim looked up from the disarray that clearly indicated an adventure of expedition proportions. We shook hands, recognizing each other from brief conversations in the main lobby and the bar at Chico.

I was in no hurry to start walking the slopes, so we ate some cold, fried grouse he plucked from the refrigerator and talked about flyfishing, the environment, music, books — the state of our well-organized lives at the moment. The sun was hot on my face sitting on the front porch. Things could stay this way for a couple of more months. I was not ready for winter. Never was.

After transferring some necessary gear from my truck to his and loading Maddy, Tim's pretty little golden retriever, we headed to some grouse covers up the drainage and into the woods. Eric Clapton played away on the cassette. The river looked dandy as it drifted off under the cloudless sky. There were deadlines to meet; they'd followed me over here and tried to catch my attention. *Screw writing*, I thought. This is more important.

We pulled off on an abandoned logging road, dust rising high above the young trees. It was hot and still and I was soon sweating (as I once mentioned to Chuck Johnson, I perspire watching football on TV). Tim was off to my right tromping through thick undergrowth and over rotting deadfalls. Maddy was coursing back and forth, bell tinkling. We worked quickly up, over, and around this piece of turf. Tim wasted little time in his hunting. Not a ball-busting egomaniac, but rather a steady, persistent hunter. I could feel the Camels and taste the beer. Good for me.

We loaded up and wound back downhill and up into the pines and aspen along another logging road. Heading up the road before jumping into the cover, we saw a ruff streak across the gap between the trees. We worked both sides of the road and turned a pair of grouse toward the end. They went streaking uphill, ground level, and I swung and missed by a mile. No more birds, but time for some water for the dog.

Anyone who thinks goldens can't work grouse should spend time with Maddy. The whole trip, she worked close-in and thoroughly, only occasionally displaying restrained disgust at my poor shooting. She was a joy in the field. Tim and his lady, JoAnne, have themselves a true friend.

After awhile we drove on to yet another cover. I learned that Tim had located several dozen over the past few years, and these were checked regularly throughout the year. This one worked up an overgrown skid trail, a path where machines dragged logs out to waiting trucks. We ducked under and stepped over a bunch of downed dog-fur lodgepole then worked up along the edges of a grassy, brushy clearing, and pushed uphill into dark woods. No birds and I was getting winded when Tim said, "Let's stop here for a bit," which was alright by me. All was silent as it usually is in big timber. We sat and rested; Maddy lay on the ground, panting slightly with full, pink-tongue extension. We worked back down to the truck (another one of them damn Toyotas) and headed into town for a few cold beers.

I offered to pay, but quickly learned that my money was no good on this trip. Tim was a hell of a guy in my eyes. The cold beer tasted of hops and yeast. My mind drifted out the window and behind the bar as I watched the river glow in the last quick-silver light of the day. Tim talked with everyone in the place. They all knew each other, and I mentally kicked myself for not spending more time in this country, land that was only two hours from home. Everyone in here seemed relaxed, happy. The mood was contagious. A fine afternoon and even a few grouse spotted.

Back at Tim's place. Dark out. Live Bob Dylan playing. Sipping some custom-designed Margaritas. Grouse on the stove filling the house with a hungry aroma. I enjoy the company of good people on a hunt as much as the country and the shooting. Talk turned, as it always does with writers and those who have been victimized by college creative writing programs, to books, places to sell stories, payment, and all too often lack of same.

I was handed an aging paperback by Craig Nova, *Turkey Hash*. A quick scan revealed tight work about ugly stuff, disenfranchised youth in California. (Later, I discovered an editor friend of mine and other writer friends who knew the guy well, and I learned that Nova liked to hunt and fish. Never know it from this harsh book. A real scary sucker.) Tim had studied writing years ago, though not as long ago as I had and had thoughts of writing for money. An ugly proposition, but something some of us must do. We don't play well with most others, are essentially unemployable. Malcontents of sophisticated dimensions.

The moon was up and close to full. The surrounding mountains wailed away in the glow. A few more drinks, and then I woke in a sleeping bag on the floor of an upstairs bedroom, sunlight kicking me awake. Another gorgeous day. Tim, Jo, and Maddy were still asleep, so I took a brief stroll.

Later we drove down to the little river and caught a few brookies and some nice rainbows in the cuts and curls and on the foam-flecked edges of deep, emerald-colored pools. Delightful action filling another clear, warm morning. The grouse were scheduled for afternoon action.

Another cover, this one running along the top of a steep hill that collapsed down to a dark creek flowing through a thickness of downed timber, small cedar, and larger pines. Maddy put up several grouse that we missed, until one jumped up into a tree and held tight. These birds behaved far differently than those of legend back in the Northeast. Those birds would fly into oblivion. These grouse frequently hid, or so they thought, in the trees. I winged a stick at the thing, watched it dash off, and then tumble to the ground from a shot by Tim. The dog took some time to find it in the matted cover. A mature, plump grouse. They lived well over here.

The afternoon slid away in a haze of excellent grouse covers and convoluted conversation. We pulled up for one last push, stepping off the road and working through an old selective cut that still had plenty of trees scattered among the downed slash and huckleberry.

A few hundred yards more, and the world was torched in a yellow-gold blaze that ignited the sky in a wide, open oval. Surrounding an old lake that over the years had turned to thick, grass marsh, towering cottonwoods were at peak color, as if on fire. It was like standing in a huge, natural stadium, the foliage looking like arc lights blazing on an autumn ball game at Wrigley Field. The explosion of color flaring against the subdued greens of the pines and the earthy tones of the undergrowth was fantastic.

We sat on a deadfall in silence. The whole scene only barely on this side of believable. This didn't seem real. It was hard to imagine that we were in the same country or even on the same planet.

"I think I'll bring Jo here tomorrow. These colors are special," said Tim.

"I know," I offered with a profundity that is locally acknowledged as pedestrian in its loftiest forms. What else could I say? We walked back to the road and the truck. Maddy was waiting. Another fine day. If they all could be like this.

We pulled into still another bar and my money still wouldn't spend, Tim springing for beers and a few shots of Jack Daniels. I *really* liked this guy. Another night of Margaritas, some rich red wine, and some venison topped with Hollandaise, my contribution to the meal. More talk about life in this sweet valley and the coming winter and a little time spent outside in the cooling night watching the moon and listening to the woods. Goddamned heaven down this way. May it always be so. A familiar prayer.

The next morning showed up on schedule, and I staggered downstairs a bit worse for the evening's wear, taking four or five months to load my gear. Tim woke, walked me to my truck and said," Let's hunt some pheasants up your way in a few weeks." We shook hands again and I headed back up into the mountains for home.

Just where the road starts its hard climb, I pulled down a minor road, stopping by a bridge that crossed a small, pocket-water stream. I rigged a light rod and caught a couple of brook trout of less than a foot, then scared the daylights out of two ruffed grouse while walking back downstream through the forest. I grabbed the gun, went back the way I came, and found the two birds holding low in a big pine. As I walked closer, they both bolted in the same direction and I missed the first and dropped the second into the hill across the creek. I got wet walking across, the water like ice. The bird looked like the one Tim shot, mature, heavy. I put it in the cooler in the back.

Earlier on the trip I had not shot to Olympic standards and I heard Tim go, "Oh shit!" when I missed an easy passing shot. There was an intensity to him that was perfectly tempered by an understanding sense of humor.

He'd have liked the two brook trout and the fact that I hit the grouse. He would have laughed quite a bit at all of this. Like I said earlier, Tim is a good guy.

Chapter Five

Sharp-Tailed Grouse

An hour or so south from Billings and just a little bit west of anywhere crowded is some fine hunting for sharp-tailed grouse. The sharps have become my steady autumn companions in a hit-or-miss fashion. Now that I know a few places to find the species east of the Continental Divide, I manage to spend a good chunk of time spraying assorted sizes of shot (usually No. 6 or No. 7 1/2) across the far reaches of the high plains and over obscure tracts of coulee and bluff country, but that's moving ahead of things a little.

Looking out from on top of a low mountain rising above the flatness, wonderful, open-ended country sails off in all directions, eventually shading dark-blue and purple in the distant haze. This is the country we will hunt, land that rides away into eternity, breaking apart in a series of motionless waves of first Ponderosa pine forest, and then sage, low cactus, and native grasses. Expansive fields of grain lead out in geometric patterns alongside creek bottoms and dry washes.

There is no hint of motion in the air. The place is soundless. The country stretches away silently, unreal, like a well-crafted relief map of gigantic proportions, not tangible rock and dirt. The towering stacks of the power-generating plant twenty miles to the east at Colstrip flash strobe light warnings to the few aircraft that wander over in that direction.

Down in the ravines winding beneath parched piles of stone that have weathered the eons of wind, sun, and cold, I am startled from an ancient reverie that traveled back to a time when no humans lived in these parts. A dozen birds rip into the bright day, wings beating swiftly. A frightened chorus of *whucker, whucker, whucker* reaches me, muted by the distance. I see puffs of smoke then hear the shooting as birds fall into the brush. I walk down the draw toward my companions, jumping members of the broken covey. Soon two of us have our limits of sharptails. It is time to move over to the next twisted drainage, to walk and daydream and maybe shoot some more.

This is empty, feral country only slightly tamed by random ranching operations. Rarely hunted and filled with grouse, pheasant, Hungarian partridge, and even a few chukars. Occasionally we sight marauding bands of Merriam's turkeys bound for who knows where in a fast-stepping, gobbling trot that kicks up small funnels of dust in the bone-dry stillness. They disappear in moments, scattering into the pines.

There is public land to hunt and some outfitters hold leases on dozens of sections amounting to hundreds of thousands of acres. And if the birds were not here in healthy numbers, the time spent with friends roaming within the timelessness would be hours well spent, though they'd be sun-baked, wind-burned, and bone-chilled, depending on the time and mood of the day.

The past week was spent autumn-wandering outside on a grand scale of near-perfect dimensions. Earlier we chased grouse in the open Crop Program land that seems to stretch out forever around here. And we'd cast over some big rainbows and browns while floating the nearby Bighorn River that cuts a dignified if slightly over-fished course through the bluffs and flats.

Either the birds or the trout would have been sufficient unto themselves, but when I happen upon both, life is sweet. Such is the way of things on this trip — plenty of grouse, a few Huns, and some nice fish that rise aggressively to dry flies. The end of the warm weather feeding binge was underway, marked by careless, steady rises. The trout were easy marks at this time of the year as they strove to build caloric reserves for a dark, fast-approaching winter — a flimflam con attracting lazy flyfishers from all over the country.

Flyfishing is part of my bird hunting and vice-versa. I read a survey in one magazine devoted to trout that indicated that close to seventy percent of all anglers were also bird hunters. Both disciplines require some degree of coordination and quick reactions. Shooting a fifty-foot cast to a working trout while you are floating rapidly away from the target is a lot like vectoring in on sharptails when they burst into the air, streaking for distant cover. It's *all* hunting when you come down to it. After one full day's hunting and fishing, tired but looking forward to cocktails and a good steak, we rolled back through wheat fields turned silver-white in the glare of the rising moon, now almost full. Deer browsed along the road. The lights of town sparkled a few miles away. Coming down off the bluffs to the gentle valley was like landing in another time zone or perhaps another planet. The road ran smoothly and the Jeep ran quickly as we hummed along at eighty-five or more.

That evening over a little bourbon and amid casual talk, we pretty much figured that life was awfully good out here in the West — good friends, interesting conversation (at least in the early going), some grouse, and confused trout leaping around for the hell of it. We were all easy and easy to please at this point in the proceedings and planned on staying that way.

The next morning broke clear, cloudless, a replica of the other ones. We piled into our vehicle for a drive southeast of Hardin to a land of alien-looking mountains and high, rolling plains that floated away into infinity with staggering durability. The country changed infinitesimally from one year to the next. The coulees eroded a little deeper, the creeks cut into the earth some, and the hills wore down imperceptibly.

Tomorrow we would hunt over east of Interstate 90 beneath the Little Wolf Mountains, but today we pitched extraneous gear in our motel rooms and struck out to a ranch with thousands and thousands of acres of land that stretched away untouched in the shadow of the Big Horn Mountains.

Somewhere between Lodge Grass and Wyola, way back from the frenetic interstate, we pulled into the ranch we were going to hunt. The owner directed us up a dirt road that climbed quickly onto a sere bench that crested for miles, running north and south. There were tended fields of grain and hay, draws choked with thick brush, and a pleasant little creek sliding along below (a

stream we learned later that held five-pound trout that were sometimes caught by the few who cast a fly to them — a local, watery
legend that was a well-kept secret).

We get out and stretch, really taking our time putting on
boots, checking and loading guns, mainly savoring the view and an
autumn day that was special anywhere, but stone-cold magic out
here. Fall and temperatures in the eighties, no wind, only small
change past noon. We all agree that our timing is right in the pocket for a birdless day, but this is nice country and we could walk
some with our guns, couldn't we?

We work right down at the edge of the bench, where the
land drops away to that small stream holding its big-trout secrets.
Some air moves languidly, without force, but we fail to kick up any
grouse. And pushing down one draw then up part of another is hot
business, and we are sweating in less than an hour. Consensus
reigns and we decide to walk out of the cover and then head back
to the rig. A real dedicated bunch on this bluebird day.

The heat and the muffled sounds of the others trudging
along the steep sides of the ravine and a few flies doing a half-
assed job of annoying me are a well-remembered, bird-hunting
rhythm that is swiftly blown away as dozens of sharptails rocket
out of the thick, thorny growth in the center of the draw. The beating wings pummel the air and vibrate in my gut. As big a group as
I've ever seen. The grouse are everywhere, flying singly and in
groups to cover up ahead. I barely manage to raise my gun and
swing the barrels at the grouse. The sun has hammered an infrared
voodoo dullness into my head, eroding reflexes. But one bird falls
and the others drop a pair of birds each. We retrieve these with
some difficulty. We don't have dogs. The downed sharps are scattered deeply in the tall, browning grass and thistle. We also kept
good marks on where the rest of the sharps landed.

Then we fan out uphill to flush the birds again. They break
in 360 degrees, busting out all over the place, forcing two of us to
pass on decent shots while the other two hit a pair each, the birds
dropping down and away in the sky, falling through the background of the purple-haze Big Horns riding the far horizon.
Exciting, fun shooting with so many grouse, picking a target is
almost difficult because of the wild abundance of the birds filling

the air all around us. You have to aim at them, though, or you will not hit anything using a scattergun approach even if you *are* using a scattergun.

Another hour passes this way and finds us back at the truck field-dressing the grouse and mostly talking about nothing much, which always seems to hold tones of lofty profundity after the shooting that was really easy work marked by the quickly fading memory of hot walking. The sun is almost gone in the west, and the air holds a chill. The ground gives up its warmth in a hurry at this time of the year, and a breeze drifts by us gliding downhill. There are cocktails and grilled steaks waiting for us back at the ranch house. We're ready. It's time to unwind.

In the morning we'd strike out for the severe emptiness of those Little Wolf Mountains between Hardin and Colstrip, searching for more sharptails. It is really hot and very dry this early into the upland season, but most of this area receives scant hunting pressure. The action has been steady bordering on very good throughout the trip.

The now-full moon is making a normally dark motel parking lot look like strange daylight, even though it is around midnight. You do not have to be a rocket scientist to know that our luck is going to hold up under the strain of our expectations. Tomorrow will be perfect. We stand in a loose circle, talking, reluctant to end the day.

The Crow Indians and others survived, actually flourished, for centuries before sociopathic trappers and Custer ripped through Native lands. The tribe is still hanging on and you see members moving along dusty roads and working at gas stations — here and there — in towns like Crow Agency and Indian Arrow. There hasn't been much else for them to do. But times are changing slowly, and whites are not quite as unpopular a tune on the Reservation or, for that matter, on the neighboring Northern Cheyenne Reservation. Tourists dollars are universally accepted as easy pickings, and the concept is catching on with the Indians.

There are three types of land holdings that concern the hunter: tribal, belonging to all Crow members; individual tribal member holdings; and private, deeded land owned by non-tribal members, like the benchland we hunted yesterday. There are also minor permutations on these basic three situations. Ranchers, guides, and outfitters, in a rare example of unanimity, all agree that a prudent individual steers well clear of tribal land, even the private holdings of individual members who may be willing to grant outsiders access. There is still too much emotion and suspicion swirling around here regarding non-tribal members and their motives regarding Crow country. There are many sections of deeded land and, despite the expansive nature of the reservations, even more non-reservation acreage lies out here waiting for bird hunters. As on the Blackfeet Reservation, a growing number of tribal members have recognized the value of sportsmen. In time, the situation regarding access will no doubt change for the better with more land opened to all of us. Patience.

The morning is already growing warm under the encouragement of another cloudless sky as we absent-mindedly kick at the dirt of a small turnout a mile off the Interstate while waiting for our guide, who pulls up in a banged-up pickup and a cloud of dust. Soon pavement gives way to yellow-colored dirt road as we wind through rugged hills of thick sandstone capped with red clinker. Ponderosa pine covers much of the hills.

The lead truck skids sideways to a halt, the two occupants hopping out, running to the other side of the road, then pointing into the gully and talking animatedly with arm gestures about something or other. We stop, get out, and quickly pick out the flock of turkeys that must number fifty, sixty birds that are now running with serious haste into forested cover. The toms are big, some look to be more than twenty pounds, and sport beards of six inches, at least. Several more groups of similar size are spotted during the rest of the morning as we wind along seldom-used backroads. Turkeys are now showing up at an alarming rate in my wanderings around Montana.

Behind us the sound of huge earth-moving equipment grinds, rattles, and rumbles. Cables from a mammoth dragline arc across the horizon. This is coal country, open-pit strip mining on a scale that is difficult to grasp. Even when you stare at the earthy labor for hard minutes, the scope is too big to fathom. Chunks of black rock the size of Buick Roadmasters are scooped up by machines that dwarf the men inside them. The tires are taller than basketball hoops. The engines belch thick, brown-black clouds of exhaust.

There is sufficient coal lying just below the fragile topsoil around these parts to power the nation for centuries, but when the black mineral finally plays out, what remains? The megalomaniacal power companies claim loudly and often that the earth can be reclaimed, returned to exactly the way it used to be prior to the mining intrusion. There are plans and schematics and blueprints slammed down on tables as exhibits to prove this cabalistic consortium's claims at raucous, rancorous public meetings held around the state over the years. The gatherings are all show and forceful venting of spleens, but they signify nothing at all in the grand money-making scam of things. A sad display, and what's been done to the countryside is beyond sad. It's tragic. Hideous.

Yes, there have been some small pieces of land temporarily reclaimed from the colossal diggings. Put enough water and fertilizer on the ground and, sure, something will sprout and appear to flourish, at least for a short time. But a lot of habitat has also been destroyed. Only the coming years will tell whether or not man has screwed up the delicate master plan out here.

We whip over the crest of a hill and plummet abruptly down, braking wildly onto a dirt-path situation that dies away into the trail we are to take in eager pursuit of the sharptails. World-class snake country in these fields, and I forgot my snake-proof chaps. No big deal. Ten minutes into the hunt one of us does a lunging, lurching pirouette at the sound of a rasping, rattling snake buzz. The creature is blown away by the guide's 12-gauge. He does not like snakes in the least, we learn.

A couple of hours of no grouse and only a few not yet in-season pheasants that fly up in a flash of reds, greens, golds, and browns. Frustrating not to be able to shoot at them. All of this combines to create a barely discernible negative attitude among us, but this drifts away over lunch.

A stock pond of several acres lies just behind the open-side barn we lounge in, eating lunch out of the sun. The ranch owner says to "give it a shot," so I assemble my six-weight, a real battered Orvis travel rod (I used to think it was a bit too stiff. Now it acts a bit sloppy, as we all do on occasion as the years roll by), tie on a hopper — it's warm so the choice seems appropriate — and walk down to the water. The line unfurls out over the water and the bug lands on the still surface. I wait for the small ripples to die a concentric death before twitching the thing — just like fishing for largemouth bass. Out of the depths, a large rainbow rises up and pounces on the fly. I set the hook and the bite of the sharp metal triggers a bouncing, tail-flapping display of anger and confusion that culminates with a high-pitched *ping* of the tippet popping from too much strain, provided by the trout and too much pressure on my part. Several more casts turn two more fish that also escape and finally one trout of twenty inches or so.

"Nice work, Holt. One out of four. Twenty-five percent. At least that's better than your attendance record in college."

And this guy is my friend, but such is life.

Soon it starts feeling hot out here, under a burning sun in a land that seemed smooth and benign when glassed from the ridgetop earlier. It doesn't feel that way now. More like a sauna. Time to walk up some more coveys, though finding grouse in these conditions seems unlikely.

Small puffs of alkali soil curl up around my boots before settling softly onto clumps of cactus and parched grass. More than a few miles of walking and no birds. Thoughts of, "Why am I here?" and, "Let's call it a day" start bouncing around in my head.

Pausing to rest on a slab of eroded sandstone, I see two of my companions working an overgrown, curving slice in the landscape, and then I see them raise their guns and swing on targets, unseen from where I sit. Guns are already being lowered as the sounds of shooting reach me. Renewed by the excitement of this action and the prospect of some more, I quickly make my way down the parched drainage in time to see several grouse stuffed into hunting vest game pouches. As on the previous bench, what seemed to be a lifeless place suddenly changed into a setting where every draw, clump of bushes, and line of tall grass adjacent to stubbled alfalfa fields was holding sharptails.

There are birds all over the place and the shooting is constant, the smell of gunsmoke hanging on the still air. We push our way through the thick grass that is knee-deep and resistant, like the heavy, wet snow of a late-February storm. The grouse take flight with loudly pounding wings, hanging tight to cover, dipping and swooping over, under, and around tree limbs, bushes, and rotting fence posts, only to burst into view, briefly flashing in the sun. Sudden opportunities vanish sharply as soon as they present themselves. In what seems like but a moment, the afternoon's hunting is done.

Again, what felt like drudgery an hour ago is shaded with burnished golden overtones that will develop and mature in the course of numerous charged regalings and retellings to friends over cognac and Jamaican cigars during the lifeless cold of winter. There will be a warm fire laughing in the background, and the dog will be asleep, not interested in the story.

At the end of this day, winter seems much closer, as it does at the end of every day in the field during the fall, but the shooting has partially diminished my dread associated with the effort of bat tling through long months of ice and too-short periods of daylight. Chasing grouse predictably works this magic each season.

To do nothing but prepare my home for the approaching northland storm blastings that will inevitably sweep down on my valley would be like hanging out on death row with no hope for a commuted sentence. A bleak prospect. Upland bird hunting is an elegant example of divine vice turned necessity.

On the drive back to our rooms, the sun is now down. We stop in the middle of a dirt road to look one last time at the land we hunted. A huge moon makes its rogue appearance over the horizon, big and ghostly but still small in the limitless space. The sweet scent of sage drifts on the evening breeze, and still there is no sound and there are no artificial lights anywhere. Except for the road, the land is the way it's always been. We're alone and no one says anything. There's no need for words. You could disappear for a long time out in this country looking for grouse while possibly tripping over a few moments of temporary sanity.

One of the main reasons for the abundance of sharptails throughout much of the West is the fact that the species is able to take advantage of all sorts of cover, seemingly the rougher and thicker, the better. Similar species are either now long gone or on their way, birds like the lesser and greater prairie chicken, heath hen, and pinnated grouse. They were far more specific concerning food and cover, and were probably not nearly as territorial as the sharptail.

While both sharps and prairie chickens evolved from essentially the same environment, mainly native prairie grass lands, sharptails have learned to take advantage of planted grains, overgrown ditches, and old structures without suffering as severely from the resulting loss of indigenous plants and somewhat alien surroundings. The sharp's range extends all the way to the Arctic Circle in Alaska. They are found in Alberta and Saskatchewan, far to the east along Hudson Bay, and in Idaho, Wyoming, on south to Nebraska, and Utah. In Montana, they are found throughout the eastern two-thirds of the state except for some stretches in the northeast quadrant that are too rough for all but mule deer, snakes, and surly arachnids. They are also scattered about in isolated pockets of dry grassland above Eureka, around the Flathead Indian Reservation, and east of Missoula, all three locations lying west of the Continental Divide.

Sharps have been known to out-compete pheasants and prairie chickens for disputed habitat, displaying a good deal more aggression when it comes to staking out and holding onto suitable ground. The bird's spring strutting and dancing ritual is similar to that of the sage grouse, though not as elaborate, and the males' neck sacs are purple compared to yellow-green for sage grouse.

Sharptails run between fifteen and twenty inches, somewhat larger than both lesser and greater prairie chickens. They also tend to be paler in color with more brown speckling and more white plumage. White spotting about the wings is conspicuous in flight. Like ruffed grouse, telling males from females in flight is difficult.

I've found sharptails in brushy coulees, alongside and in grain fields, along creek bottoms and nosing around in Ponderosa pine forests. The birds take advantage of whatever is available. What appears prime habitat may be birdless, while identical cover just over the ridge will be packed with several dozen grouse. And in some covers, this lifeless vs. abundant situation has played itself out year after year. In other locales, the birds are where you find them, and this varies wildly from year to year; they are inconsistent in this respect. Grassy hills with shallow draws of brush and berry are always worth a look as are creek drainages given over to dense grass and bushes. Toward evening and early in the morning, the edges of wheat, alfalfa, and hay fields are productive. Also, just after sunrise, if you listen, you will often hear the birds cackle as they start moving around toward feed. Sharps will roost in trees; where there is tall brush or bush, they will often hold well off the ground, making for quicker shooting. Small dips and depressions in fields also provide cover. Machinery is unable to cut down into these declivities, sparing the grouse from an ugly death. Like most upland birds, sharptails love to hang out around abandoned farm buildings. There is shelter from the weather and predators and usually an abundance of food and some water nearby. Ideal terrain.

The bottom line is that finding the birds can often take time, but when you do, there are usually quite a few grouse present, especially as the season progresses. Again, as with most upland species, they tend to travel only short distances on the first flush or if they've been lightly hunted so far during the year.

When the grouse are holding tight in brushy pockets of wild berries and rosehips and nasty stuff like chokecherries, a good flushing dog can save the day. Walking by yourself or with a couple of others can be frustrating in the extreme in this habitat. I've walked right over birds on my own, only to have a decent covey burst from the same stuff the next day when hunting with a dog. The birds run like track stars in this stuff, too.

Early one season just after dawn, a rare appearance at this hour on my part, we reached the fields we were to hunt this cloudy, slightly damp morning. The wheat had been knocked down to stubble. Thick grass, waist high, bordered the grain, and a steep-sided coulee filled with nasty-looking brush and mangled-looking thorn trees ran in a jagged path paralleling the area.

As we got ready, we heard a number of the sharptails talking away about a quarter-mile distant, perhaps a little more. We turned the dogs loose and started quick-stepping our way to the birds. The dogs both got birdy immediately but broke off, moving quickly ahead. Old scent. We called the dogs back in, and they jumped a decent covey right where we thought it should be. The birds broke up head high, then dove quickly down toward the tangled safety of the coulee, making abrupt calls of alarm. My friend doubled easily. Mornings were easier for him. I hit one right in front of me that was blown forward several feet by the force of the shot. I missed wildly on another. We worked along the edges of the coulee and the dogs put up grouse steadily, though they flew farther each time and then seemed to run for the border, based on the next takeoff point.

Within a couple of hours of easy walking, we had limited out. Actually, my friend was finished in half the time, but tagged along giving me all sorts of grief about all kinds of shortcomings, both real and imagined.

"Sure that gun fits you, John?"

"Yes."

"Fooled me. How about those boots, a little tight around the tendons, there. You're kind of lurching along. How's your head? Does it ache?"

"My gun may not fit, but it's loaded," I mentioned. "And I never listen to anyone who thinks that Donahue or Oprah or Geraldo have any redeeming value."

"Hey, they just serve as background while I'm reading or eating," and my friend was clearly wounded. I had some sort of small advantage.

"I say shoot all people who attend those atrocities in person. And finish off all game show audiences. Or ship them to another planet where such imbecilic trash is considered worthwhile."

"How about the hosts? You want to waste them, too?"

"Hell no. They're the damn magnets that draw the subnormals in from under the viaducts and out of the video arcades," I offered. "They're of marginal value, sort of like local sportscasters. They keep the idiots herded up." Admittedly, this is a subject that has very little to do with bird hunting, but I was carrying a 20-gauge and one could dream, at least, and talk does range far and wide while out in the open. "Besides, I think Wink Martindale is a prodigious talent, right up there with Bob Ewbanks. I take that back. Nobody's as good as Bob, and what a genuine smile he has."

"I'm beginning to agree with the others, John. You *do* need help."

"Thanks."

We continued hunting and the day turned wet and miserable; we were soaked and cold by the time we got back to the truck. Time for some water for the dogs, then a warm drive into town for a cheeseburger and the home fires. I like playing outside, but not when the rain is really sleet that knifes through your clothes and skin like teeny razors. No way. I'm too old for that silliness.

Another time I'd found sharp-tailed grouse by listening in the morning for their cacklings was on a trip to just south of the Montana border below the tiny town of Quietus and above the even smaller village of Leiter, Wyoming. There were creeks running turbid in the early September drizzle. Streams with names like Hanging Woman, LX Bar, and Deadhorse. There wasn't much water in any of them, and I saw the dried remains of a bullhead or down-sized catfish stuck in some dried mud. No trout around these parts.

It was easy to get lost out here; the land all looked the same to a visitor. One hill gave way to another and still another, all of them dry, brown, sere, lifeless. And being trapped by an early winter storm would be disastrous. The roads would turn slippery, treacherous, soon impassable, but I'd gained permission to hunt sharps on this rancher's land, and I'd paid for my out-of-state permit. I was damned sure going to launch a few rounds in earnest before bailing out to the boring security of the nearby Interstate.

I'd found the place one day a few years back while researching a story for the *Denver Post* on working ranches, those operations that charge moronic dudes from the East and the Left coasts for the privilege of stacking hay, feeding cattle, mending fence, and mucking out cattle crap from huge, drafty barns. In the process, the dudes get kicked out of bed before first light, are treated like the subnormal fools they indeed are, and get to part with fairly large sums of money.

I remember asking one rancher what he thought about the whole deal and he said,"If you'd told me twenty years ago that there were people dumb enough to pay to do my work around here, I'd have said 'No fucking way.'"

You could tell the notion of a working ranch, the idea of people actually paying to do this labor, was still too new and strange to be funny. That would come in time.

Anyway, I asked, and the guy said sure, I could hunt the sharps and even the Huns and pheasants, but I hadn't seen any of those, yet. The day before, working up a dry creekbed, I'd kicked up a bunch of sharps and dropped one and then another and another as I slogged up the streambed, sinking calf-deep at times in the thick accumulation of orange-red dust that was turning to quicksand as the weather kept coming on and the moisture kept soaking the earth.

A couple of more hours and I'd be back at the truck, completing a large loop that ran up and down barren hills, sharp draws, and along grassy flats. A massive oil rig was visible just below me to the south, painted a puke green, lying on its side, waiting to be erected and set into motion. The rancher would make more money from the oil leases on his land in one year than he could turn running cattle for a decade of brutal, backbreaking work. Cattle need food all year and they don't care if it's snowing a blizzard or one-hundred-twenty degrees, mosquito hot. Hell, the oil money was easy in comparison. Tear open the envelope, endorse the check, and deposit it on the way to the bar for a few drinks. True, you had to do this once a month, but certain sacrifices simply *had* to be made.

My legs were wearing out, turning rubbery, and the storm was growing in intensity, shifting from rain, bypassing sleet, and now driving down in thick sheets of snow. I quickened the pace, the truck a pale smudge on the distant road across this small draw, over the next hill, and across a mile of sage flat. I was sliding and slipping downhill where four or five or six sharptails (who could count in this mess?) zipped into the air, their thrashing wings pounding through the storm. I braked and brought the gun up simultaneously, aiming at the highest birds and hitting the lowest as I pitched forward unexpectedly with a sudden stop. A patch of dry rock scraped clean from my skidding boot heels. I went down to pick the sharp up, and two more birds went airborne. I hit one as it climbed to the top of the far side of the drainage. The grouse fell back down the slope. The others were long gone. I shoved this one, blood dripping from its beak and neck, into the game vest and dog-trotted toward the truck.

The storm had gone berserk. I guessed where the truck was and almost ran into it, blinded by the gale that now howled like an insane owl through the brush. I was gasping and wheezing, blood pounding like a jackhammer in my ears and throbbing in my arms. Sweat was pouring down my cheeks and rolling into my eyes, burning and obscuring my vision that flickered at the throbbing of my overburdened heart. I needed a cigar. A thick, black one from Honduras. It would have to wait until I reached town, if I reached town. This was going to be quite the sporting drive. I was excited, eager. You bet.

I fired the engine, turned on the defroster full-blast, hurriedly shoved the snow off the windshield, and let out the clutch. The wheels spun crazily. I could hear mud and grit and rock ricochet around inside the rear wheelwells. Finally moving and gathering momentum, I rocked and swerved down the road at perhaps forty (the speedometer said sixty but was confused by lack of traction on the wet road). I couldn't see, and bashed into a rock with a front tire that sent the thing shooting into the skid plate with a loud *clang-carack*. I kept glancing at the oil light, figuring some sort of internal bleeding was about to occur. None did, thank the gods.

Neon lights heralded the arrival of the town of Sheridan. Making it this far safely was like finding a box stuffed with hundred-dollar bills. I pulled into some roadside gas station-grocery store travesty and filled up — unleaded. I grabbed a twelve-pack of Pabst, paid with a twenty, drove down to a drive-in liquor store and picked up a pint of schnapps. I had a room waiting for me in Hardin, seventy-five miles up the highway and figured I'd break the law with a couple of beers and a shooter or two of the sweet booze. There was no one on the snowy road, and I figured I'd go into the ditch on the right if I had to.

A black cigar of the proper dimensions was lying on the dashboard. I slid it out of its cellophane wrapper, then lit a stick match and torched the thing, clouds of dense blue smoke filling the truck's cab. The aroma was strong, reeking of fertile tropical soil and well-cured tobacco oil. Go ahead. Make them illegal — I'll still smoke one whenever I want to, and right in front of you. Call the cops. I really am concerned. I really care. Have a tofu salad on me and worship the crystal of your choice.

Back at the motel, I cleaned the birds, dumping the feathers and the guts in the wastebasket that I then set outside the door. I deposited the grouse in the cooler sitting beneath the stand that supported the TV that was now featuring Australian Rules Football. Oh boy. I washed the drying blood from my hands in a hot shower, ordered an anchovy, mushroom, green pepper, and onion pizza, then finished off the beer and schnapps. Another bird hunt reaches a safe conclusion.

One of the best sharptail hunts I ever had was on the far northeastern boundary of the Blackfeet Reservation. Not spectacular shooting by any means, but a damn good time filled with the right amounts of all of the elements that go into a memorable outing — country, people, dogs, weather, birds.

Only tribal members could shoot the sharps on the Res, so we worked right along the edge, staying on some public land that was okay to hunt. We could tell where we were by fence lines and county roads that ran north and south, the line of demarcation we were concerned with. There were tremendous populations of sharptails on Blackfeet land, and I hoped one day the tribe would change its policy and allow non-tribal members to walk the empty stretches of their wonderful land chasing these native birds. If they never do open the season, I can't say I blame them. They've been screwed big-time too often by Uncle Sam.

Joe Kipp drove us up on to a wide, undulating ridge, and we had sandwiches and chips. Joe elected to walk a ridge above us to try and spot the birds. Blanche and Chuck Johnson and I, along with their German wirehairs Cody and Annie, moved swiftly downhill, across a small earthen dam holding back scummy-looking water, and then we drifted sidehill through native grass, chokecherry, and the usual assortment of obstructions replete with rodent holes that fit our boots perfectly. I fell down immediately and Chuck followed suit a bit farther on. Chuck is one heck of a walker; I could never keep up. But if there is a hole, hidden water, or thin ice to be found within a ten-mile radius of where he is hunting, Chuck'll find it. Guaranteed. Trust me. This guy has elevated the talent to an art form. Blanche seemed fine and the dogs worked back and forth, but there were no birds.

We trudged around a large bluff, through wide-open draws, and up a tangled creekbed without success. I climbed up on the bench and watched my companions struggle below me. The dogs were like small toys moving around, and Joe was barely visibly to the north, not far from the Canadian border.

The wind blew cool and steadily up here. Where were the grouse? Maybe up here eating the grasshoppers or possibly these thick crickets that were the size of sparrows. I walked through gray and brown grass pockmarked with melting patches of rotten snow, the remnants of a storm that raced through this country a few days ago. The Rocky Mountain Front was magnificent, of course, and the isolated stands of mountains out on the plains were covered in fresh snow.

Walking slowly, I started to clean my glasses when the world exploded. At least a dozen sharptails charged into the air right at my feet, streaking low and fast for a small valley just ahead. Dropping the glasses, I fired, missing the first time, and drawing feathers on the second shot.

"Jesus. They're all over the place," I yelled, still shaking as I put the shades back on.

Chuck and Blanche crested the rise, with Chuck leading by five lengths and looking strong in the stretch. The dogs appeared and the four of them went down over the hill. I heard distant shooting and saw Cody retrieve a grouse. Kipp was now beside me and we ambled along.

"Birds surprise you a little, did they?" laughed Kipp with a jive-ass smile I knew all too well. "John, you've got to be ready for those grouse," and as he said this a pair jumped up and I covered one with an easy shot I never took, watching the sharp swing down out of range.

"I had him, but I just didn't want to shoot. Something stopped me."

"I know. It happens. Maybe you saw Chuck and Blanche in the corner of your eye and that made you stop. It doesn't matter."

"Right. Good to see birds after all this time," and I worked the top of the valley while Joe went across and to the next rise. And a single sharptail came from the side of the hill below Joe, dipping slightly over the ground that dropped away beneath it, then rising as it raced by me. I swung through the bird, pulling the trigger, and it fell quickly to the ground, trailing feathers. Annie picked it up and that was that.

Later, I shot another that disappeared into the brush or an animal hole. Cody scented the bird but couldn't turn up the grouse, either. And I was done for the day, satisfied. Joe and I worked on a keg of Black Bart beer a friend had provided for me. Chuck and Blanche hunted some more and then we sipped a bit of good scotch and said our goodbyes. The hunt was over.

Not many birds. Who cared? Fine country. The finest. Good company. The dogs worked well, and Joe was his normal wise-guy self. A perfect time in all respects.

Chapter Six

Merriam's Turkeys

I had only the vaguest idea what time it was. Very early, for sure. Certainly not five a.m. yet. The Ponderosa pines were visible as towering, multi-armed demons standing all around me in the dark. The stars were still out, shining intensely, and the first suggestions of a false dawn glowed faintly on the edges of the hills and bluffs. Long needles carpeted the ground, covering patches of lichen-covered rock and matting last year's dry grass. The spring had been unseasonably warm and dry so far. Scant moisture had fallen, and the melting snow was long gone, soaked up by the greedy ground.

My feet crunched on the stuff, a brittle, hollow sound. Trying to find the roost tree I'd discovered yesterday was proving troublesome. The thick-trunked pine should be right around here, only a few hundred yards from my turkey camp, such as that was: no water, a small fire ring, the back of the truck serving as a kitchen, and my sleeping bag and tarp passing for a bedroom. Austerity has a well-remembered ring, but one I'm comfortable with, whether on the road or out in the sticks.

The drive over to this sparsely populated part of southeast Montana was maybe seven hundred miles, twelve hours or more, but this location was one of the best places in the West for hunting the large birds — both in the spring and in autumn. Back home you had to put in for a turkey permit and pray for the luck of the draw if you wanted to hunt the things in the Flathead Valley. There were fewer than two hundred openings available, and the odds were long. Out this way, all you needed to do was walk into a sporting goods store in Billings or down in Sheridan and pay for

the various permits and a conservation license, a total of less than fifteen bucks this year (approximately $70 if you were from out-of-state) and an additional few dollars for the fall.

A friend had showed me this place years ago in what proved to be a hunt of heroic, slightly mad proportions (more on that later). Now I come back at every opportunity to spend a little time perched on this pine-forested bluff that looks out over miles and miles of rolling hills and eroded coulees. The varying shades of green displayed by the native grasses, small cactus, pine needles, and sage blended easily with the ochers, buffs, and subtle pinks of the rock formations and exposed earth. This was wild, unspoiled country, and I'd never seen another hunter in all the years, not even at the small store some miles distant that also served as a post office and gas station. One pickup truck barreling along the rutted path that led to turkey camp was the extent of human visitation during all of my undisciplined forays.

That was the main reason I drove all this way. To be alone, by myself. The turkeys were just an excuse, though a damn good one in my mind. I've not shot many of the Merriam's in this brief span of years, but I know where they are, to some extent. The trick is in the timing. Too early and the birds are scattered all over hell and back. Even the locals can't find the things. Show up after the spring procreational soiree has completed its bizarre dance, and the situation is similar. The turkeys are dispersed and, even if they are trotting around in the trees or strutting in the grassy meadows, they are more than a shade reluctant to come to my calls, amateur efforts at best. But when the birds are in full rut, so to speak, discordant notes bombed away from the belly of a tuba would work. Neophyte scratchings on a hollow cedar box sound like a symphony to the lovestruck turkeys. At the first annoying notes, again if the timing is right, gobblings emanate from hills in all directions. Pure lunacy. Lovely sounds singing through the air.

The roost tree I was trying to find right now was one of several I'd found in the area. Arriving in the afternoon, I set up camp, grilled a burger, and sipped a few gin-and-tonics (no limes, a Spartan trip). Around the time the sun started fading over the horizon, casting the countryside in an eerie orange-gold light, a series of *gobbles, putts,* and assorted other forms of turkey madness issued from the coulee behind me. The cacophony advanced nearer, finally culminating in the *thwack*ing of large wings beating and some disgruntled mumbling as they settled onto their perches for the night. What a crew.

I was sure I knew which tree they'd pulled into. The other three were growing along a gentle slope a half-mile away. Too far for the birds' racket to have sounded so close to camp. Tomorrow I'd shoot my turkey and then head to a small river running freely even farther in the middle of nothing where I'd try my hand at some untamed rainbows that ran to good size. Killing a couple of weeks in these parts was almost too easy.

Standing well alone in this country, looking away toward Wyoming in the south and Billings many miles north, the familiar, not unwelcome feeling of loneliness descended, another reason to be out here and away from the smothering security of civilization. Back there, it seems I never have the chance to feel anything but what I'm told or programmed to feel: Do this. Think that. Buy into another administration con. Don't step out of line. That's where the loneliness comes in handy, the feeling is a way of connecting with life, to turn briefly humble without being publicly humiliated. We all get enough of that trying to earn a living.

That's the power of this country, a place so foreign to most of us, alien to me at times, that we don't have a natural clue about what's taking place. Lightning strikes an exposed seam of coal and a smoldering fire starts, watched by no one. The coal may smoke and flare into flame, sizzling for centuries, until it is doused by heavy rain and runoff or burns its way through to the other side of the hill, or runs out of fuel. The fire is so hot, mudstone and sandstone are baked granite-hard and kiln-cured to the color of dried blood. A fifty-foot seam of coal may cook two-hundred feet of rock lying above. The clinker eventually builds up into huge beds of porous rubble storing millions of gallons of water that seep down from the efforts of wicked storms that rage above. Artificial wells naturally made. Trees and brush grow best in these spots, and wild animals know them for their water. There are several such places near camp, wild drawing cards for the Merriam's.

I built up the fire and fried a fat porkchop and some onions in butter and garlic, threw together some salad that was liberally doused with Paul Newman's famous dressing. It was all I could find at a small store some hours up the road. I was hungry and finished off the meal in minutes, then restoked the dwindling fire, ignited a cheap cigar from Connecticut, built a tall drink, and enjoyed the night. Coyotes howled away from the surrounding ridges, talking to each other. They knew the turkeys were here, too. Earlier, I'd heard a few calls from the packs, then some miles off, as the birds began to roost. I'd have some competition, but hopefully the dogs weren't armed. Climbing into the sleeping bag, I tried to make sense out of the sky, but my mind faded to black and I was out until maybe four. Now I was trying to find that damn roost tree and a place to hide.

The stars were disappearing, and the sky in the east was actually turning to soft blue when I found the tree. The ancient pine, several feet thick at the base, gnarled and twisted from its long life, hundreds of years to be sure, loomed above me a hundred yards away, thick roots clinging to thin soil and crumbling sand-stone ledges.

Dark, lumpy objects, a lot of them, were hunkered down on limbs twenty or more feet up. As quietly as possible, I crept toward a downed pine, its bark black and the exposed wood weathered gray. The cover was less than forty yards from the birds. Crouching down, I crawled back into an opening in the branches and situated myself so that I had a shot through a man-sized window in the limbs. Sitting on my butt, knees drawn to my chest, I rested the shotgun, an old Savage .22/20-gauge, in the space between my legs. I was afraid to move or make any noise, but cautiously practiced sighting in on where I thought the turkeys would land in just a few minutes. They are notorious early risers.

Long moments passed and my mind wandered far into the coulees. I wondered what it was like living out here all year as a homesteader. The climate was extreme, fluctuating crazily between searing heat and teeth-cracking cold — no wind in summer and fierce gales in winter, sleet and dust choking the periods in-between. What a way to go. What drove men to leave the safety of towns and cities to risk starting a new life out in this desolation? I knew the answer, for me at least.

There was freedom in this frightening vastness. A chance to do what I wanted by myself with no one looking over my shoulder. Knowing that what happened, happened, and the consequences be damned, was intoxicating. Yes, I knew why I would have taken a chance on this country, and I could understand the unexplained drive in others a hundred years ago.

The sky was now a washed-out robin's-egg blue across the horizon. The lumps in the old tree were stirring, making small sounds. Not clucks or purts or anything like that, more like the first sounds a person makes when he rides up out of a deep sleep.

I readied the gun and breathed shallowly. Then the turkeys started dropping out of the trees in the growing light. They sounded like sacks of cement hitting the ground, and it was not a vision blessed with gracefulness. The birds didn't bounce; rather, they went *thump* then tried standing on stiff legs, shaking their feathers and tentatively working big wings.

I was reminded of a game where I saw a former Chicago Cubs'player, Dave Kingman, rounding second base, arms wind-milling, long legs pumping as he gallantly tried to stretch a double into a leg (very leggy) triple. He slid and never reached third, tagged dead out by the length of a Rolls-Royce. The crowd howled, then cheered at the unconscious audacity of the effort. A Chicago sportswriter once described Kingman running the bases to the effect that he looked like an empty paint can being tossed from the window of a car doing sixty on a bumpy road. I stifled a laugh. That's how these turkeys looked: ungainly, not really with the pro-gram.

In a minute or so, a disorderly group of the birds milled about in the dead grass that was giving way to new, fresh green sprouts. I'd never seen this many males together, did not know if the hens roosted with them. I doubted this. Breeding was a con-tentious act of horny territoriality. I sighted in on two males, trying to determine the largest. They were both huge, well over twenty pounds, with long beards, blue-white heads giving way to ugly, dusty-red wattles hanging from their chins and necks.

I knew the .22 would kill either with a head shot, but I was unsure of my ability to hit what I aimed at. I was excited and shaky. I flipped the selector to the lower barrel, loaded with a three-inch magnum ("Magnooms"as a friend calls them) 20-gauge filled with copper-plated No. 2s. Upland birds, yes, but more like big game. A lot of energy is needed to drop a Merriam's with a flank shot. The turkey on my left walked a few yards closer and gave me an angled profile. A regal bird now standing dead still. I aimed at an area at the base of the neck and fired.

Boom! The concussion rocked through the coulees and over the bluffs. The turkeys ran, leaped for the air, and made sounds I'd never heard out of a bird before. Yelps, gagging gobbles, and strained clucks. An avian Chinese fire drill. On the ground was my turkey, on its side, one wing beating a dying tune.

I stood up, almost falling back down, legs gone stiff with the waiting. I was wired, high on adrenaline, and weaved my way the short distance to the fallen creature. The others in the flock were gone. Out of sight and sound. I'd hit this one with a number of pellets in the neck, making a ragged, bloody mess. The shoulder and wing were damaged as well, though I doubted these wounds would have done in the bird. I set the gun in the grass and lifted the Merriam's by the legs. It felt heavy, like a brace of very big channel catfish.

I let out a scream that had atavism written all over it and just looked at the huge bird. That yell and all I could think was, "What a huge Goddamned turkey." One of the highest things I'd ever done outdoors, and all I could think was, "What a huge Goddamned turkey."Moments of such profundity are stark, raving amazing, aren't they?

Walking back to camp with the bird slung over my shoulders, wings extended, I could feel the waning heat of the animal through my vest and shirt. Field dressing it was anticlimatic. I left on one foot and a complete leg attached for purposes of sex identification in case I happened upon a game warden. Fat chance. The tail feathers — large, mottled bronze, black and tan with a few hints of gray — were stowed carefully in a large freezer bag, souvenirs for my children and potential wings for grasshoppers I would tie for late-summer flyfishing. I hung the bird so that it cooled quickly in the morning air, then wrapped it in a couple of thick garbage bags before storing it in a cooler filled with block and cubed ice.

I made some dense black coffee, Golden Sumatran, added a dash or two of bourbon, and toasted the turkey, the country, the day, and my good fortune. If only all hunts were like this one. Again, fat chance, but I was a happy boy at the moment. Coyotes were barking on the ridges. They must have winded the turkeys, and I heard a lone gobble way off to the west away from the dogs. I'd take a nap and then break camp. The rainbows were calling me now.

Wild turkeys bear little resemblance to the anemic, white-feathered morons raised commercially, the often sad birds we slice up for Thanksgiving and Christmas. The real ones run as fast as horses, see and hear many, many times better than humans, and are smarter and hardier than the domestic version. Anything that can live in this country through all of the heat and cold and wind and drought has got to be tough. Outwitting marauding packs of coyotes is no easy thing, either. Imagine trying to call in a mate during the spring breeding season. Sure, a hen or two may show up willing and eager, but the coyotes follow these sounds right to their source. They're a dead giveaway indicating an easy meal. Bodies charged with sexual lust and the stress of defending territory, screwing for a turkey must be demanding, nerve-wracking work.

The wild birds I've eaten tasted like no store-bought turkey I ever cooked. The meat is sweet, tasting of the country, of the pine nuts the birds love. And their flesh has not been tough or stringy, but rather, satisfyingly resistant, like pheasant or ruffed grouse.

Breasting out a Merriam's, then marinading the meat in a mixture of red wine, Jamaican jerk (a peppery spread), and a few garlic cloves is the first step toward gourmandish heaven. Rubbing the breasts with a little extra-virgin olive oil and then quickly searing the flesh close over hot coals moves you nearer. The meat is then cooked carefully, farther above the fire, until well-heated all the way through. Maybe a couple Idaho bakers are sizzling in the coals wrapped in foil. Slabs of the breast meat and the potato loaded with butter and sour cream (the meat's lean anyway) and all of this washed down with a case of Merlot —"Let me go, Lord. It's all downhill from here."

I have no concrete idea how big these turkeys get. Rumors of twenty-eight, even thirty-two pounders run through the coulees, but a twenty-four-pound Merriam's is considered a large bird. Males run around forty-eight inches and females about thirty-six. Regardless, the toms have knife-like spurs on their legs used for protection and for arbitrating internecine squabbles. The thought of an angry turkey running at me with the speed of Secretariat, spurs armed, is daunting. I'll pass on the experience.

The birds are native to the West (and many portions of the East, Midwest, and Southeast), particularly the Southwest and Mexico, but their numbers were decimated in years past from overhunting and loss of habitat due to farming, ranching, and development. Better management practices and reintroduction has seen the birds come back all over Montana. There are several flocks roaming casually along roads near my home in the northwest corner of the state. They stop traffic on busy highways as they amble across the thoroughfare, and they are always bothering a neighbor's guinea fowl, with what purpose in mind, no one can guess. A friend of mine shot one last spring with a bow. He was quite pleased as he should have been. All I know is that the birds are around and they are wild bordering on slightly crazed, an element that rubs off on most of my hunts or would-be hunts.

And there are the turkey hunts that never see a turkey, birdless wonders, like the one Bob Jones, Tim Joern, and I took in April, again in the southeast corner of the state a few miles above Wyoming, one of my favorite places in the world.

Tim and I left Whitefish late in the afternoon, stopping briefly to fish the Blackfoot River before climbing over MacDonald Pass. Rotten snow was still piled up on the sides of the highway. Bands of elk were feeding in the dead fields of grass on the slopes above us. Then we dropped steeply through the mountains, running quickly through Helena, down alongside the Missouri River to I90.

Three hours later, after buying gas and more cigarettes, we followed the highway as it climbed up through the rimrocks guarding the Yellowstone River. The lights of the city of Billings and oil refineries with their tall stacks belching bright yellow flames of wasted natural gas — all of this foolishness blazed behind us. Another hour and we turned east on a less grand stretch of pavement, passing the Little Bighorn Battlefield. An hour more, and we eased down an even narrower road of rock and dirt.

It was closing in on midnight so we pulled over and had a beer. The sky, always the insane Montana sky, screamed with stars so far away. Emptiness, but never enough to keep me happy. After more miles we cut across a high plateau aiming ever eastward toward turkey country. Deer eyes glowed in the glare of our headlights, white-orange globes hanging in the air. The country was green, fresh, the air frigid, we could see this in the arcs. At the bottom of a draw at a wye, I managed to get us lost. Headed in the wrong direction, we finally pulled into a little village that straddled a small river.

The place was closed for the night, but looked neat and strangely illuminated in the wide halos of blue-white yard lights. There was a disturbing hint of yuppiness to the homes. They were too well-kept for this part of the state. Freshly painted picket fences (an awful show), trimmed lawns, no beater cars passed out on cement blocks. Something wasn't right. Had the joint been discovered, given way to New Age silliness, specialty coffees, and knick-knack boutiques? We hoped not.

Turning around, we followed the winding road as it paralleled the river. Tall bluffs glowing weirdly in the moonlight, and marked by striated layers of different-colored sediments compacted into rock over the millennia closed in on us. I was sure we were headed straight this time, but Tim had his doubts. Finally, I recognized an old battered cattleguard, and we clattered across, pulling into the riverside campground after two a.m. We were beat.

After unloading several tons of provisions, Tim quickly built a snug nest in the back of his truck and was soon snoring away. I built a drink and then another. Following the hangover dregs of a long winter, the atmosphere felt charged with magic, like a gift from heaven, to once again be back in this country. The intervening six months since I'd been here last October hunting sage grouse and the turkeys had never existed. The place was timeless, sweeping me totally into the sweet void of uncluttered wildness. Finally, I climbed into my sleeping bag; making a pillow out of a duffel, I nodded off. La-la land was eagerly awaiting my return. It could have me, at least for a few hours.

The sun woke me. Tim, having done the hard work of driving, was taking advantage of some well-earned downtime, an unconscious vacation. As the day warmed, I went down to the river, stripped, and waded into the ice-cold stream. I could hear the flow of dark water rushing through the large gate of the dam a mile above. Hundreds of carp, fins turned scarlet in spawning intensity, worked in the shallows. Mule deer trotted away at the sight of the bone-white human splashing with moronic delight. The animals vanished over the hills.

Drying off, I felt great, awake again, and I brewed some coffee (a specialty blend, I must admit), organized camp to some extent, and then poured some orange juice. We weren't going to be shooting today, merely casting large streamers to pools, runs, and riffles in hopes of tagging one of the big, rare browns that swam here or maybe a smallmouth bass or a couple of sauger. What we caught, if anything, was unimportant. Being here was the deal.

As I finished off the juice, Bob pulled up in a rented car, having made the early morning run up from U-Cross where he was a writer-in-residence researching a novel. We grinned and shook hands, exchanging hellos and, "Damned good to see you again" greetings. The coffee was hot and Tim rose with the sound of our talking. More introductions and the day was off and running.

We talked away an hour, headed up to the dam, and caught nothing. Time for some beer, and then we fished the river and caught nothing. Too hot and no clouds and low water. My friends doubted my tales about the browns (much to my relief, later that year Gary LaFontaine released a book, *Proven Patterns*, that also mentioned the big trout swimming in this river. I was off the hook. I'd popped the strong tippet of disbelief). Tim went up to the reservoir to fish, and Bob and I talked about hunting turkeys, ducks, big game, about professional sports — especially motor sports — and burned in the spring's new sun.

Tim returned, fishless and discouraged, but a drink or two brought him around, and soon we had a dinner fire going. The meal proved to be an exotic feast: Alligator, provided by Tim, seasoned with red pepper and augmented with baked potatoes. All of this was delicately washed down with some fine wine I'd brought for the occasion — Thunderbird with a metal screw cap, the green jug still in its brown bag. We were living once again.

To be honest, as darkness heightened, we were all a bit hammered. The next thing I knew, Bob and I were following Tim to the river. He was carrying a matte-black-finish 10-gauge loaded with 3 1/2-inch magnums. Tim wanted a carp or to make some noise or whatever. The report of that first shot was like a howitzer in the still night. The explosion shot flame several feet beyond the barrel.

"Good God! That will sure as hell knock over a turkey,"Bob offered, and we laughed and headed back to camp for some sleep.

We broke camp with hangover intensity and mounted up. We drove into turkeyville from the backside along a wide-open road that drifted through rolling grass country studded with eroded sandstone towers. We stopped so Tim could cut off the head of a road-killed porcupine. He was a science teacher and loved to bring back these rotting trophies for his class. Photos were taken, none that would ever see the light of print, but so what?

A gravesite marked with plastic flowers, weird sculptures of nothing recognizable, and a sign saying that"the damn bank killed my husband,"highlighted the trip. Then abruptly the openness gave way to stands of Ponderosa, and we ground up through massive abutments of weathered, yellow sandstone. Another couple of miles and we were at camp, the place unchanged since last autumn.

After setting up tents and scattering gear with no particular plan in mind, we went off in different directions looking for sign of the turkeys. All I found were some old, ratty feathers and a carcass, the work of coyotes, and some dried droppings the thickness of fat pencils. I didn't hear a gobble. Usually the birds were calling all over the place. The spring, though hot, was running three weeks or so late. The birds were not around, adding to the brown-trout disbelief.

But we carried on, Bob and I talking away, Tim napping. A storm blew darkly over the country, spitting a few wind-driven drops, and we moved closer to the fire. And then we looked and listened some more for the Merriam's. Nothing. Not a sound. Time for some dinner then the late night, blazing-fire talk that wandered the course of music, hunting, fishing, and politics, though this last subject received scant attention. Someone tripped over a stone in the dark and fell into the fire for a second, which livened things up, then the conversation took off on less-traveled tangents and the evening passed into sleep.

That morning we gave up on the birds. We were too early. The hunting was a dead issue, so we headed off to Ashland to look for a Northern Cheyenne cemetery, more research for Bob's book. In town we stopped at the Office Bar (the Office, in Ashland?) and

talked with some tribal members over beers. There was an under-
current of, "Why are you white assholes in here?" and I felt uneasy.
Paranoid? I don't think so, but who knows? Bob exchanged hats
with someone and struck up a conversation with a woman named
Yellow Eyes. I suggested that it was time to head out of Dodge. We
beat a disciplined but hasty retreat back out into the street.
Somewhere during the course of the bar visit, Tim obtained directions to a ranch. The wife was generous with her information,
directing us to thick cover along a small creek. She said there were
turkeys working in a nearby field.

In an astounding display of hunting fervor, Tim donned
camo clothing in the time it took Bob and myself to grab our guns,
and just as swiftly, he had us positioned in amongst thick brush
and tall grass. Cottonwoods blocked the cloudy sky.

Tim used a diaphragm call and we thought we heard some
gobbles. Breaking out to the edge of the field, we saw the birds. A
dozen huge turkeys feeding a quarter-mile away. We crouched
down and worked closer, and then closer yet. The birds were still
there, barely moving. We crept through the brush, moving in for
the kill. Peering through a thicket, we saw the turkeys. Not moving
and for good reason. The flock was a bunch of downed, black
trunks and limbs. Easy shots but not what we were after.

Onward and upward and we found ourselves wandering
the Bighorn Battlefield. More research and a few photographs, then
we parted with Bob (I'd be back in a week fishing the Bighorn with
him). Tim and I camped along a river that cruised with big-fish
intent a few hours from Helena. Once again we built a fire and
talked away the night. Rain woke me the next morning, the stuff
soaking my bag and drenching my face. Tim was out cold in the
truck. Sandhill cranes were clacking away in the fields along the
stream, killing time before they lifted off to breeding grounds farther north, much farther, up in Alberta, in the flat, pothole-marsh
country. I longed to fly away with them. I rigged up a flyrod and
caught some browns, a glorious time, and then we headed home.

No turkeys. Not even the sight of one, but a great trip in my
eyes. Tim grumbled some. He had a right to — he'd done the driving and put up with a fishless river and a turkeyless camp. But a

month later, we were back on the road chasing trouble and trout and a good time. Time heals most wounds.

Many people would have been depressed at the lack of action, bird-wise. I wasn't. Bob and I have spent a bit of time together chasing trout and birds, but we know that being outside is the goal; the rest was gravy. I'd never traveled with Tim before and hoped he wasn't upset. He wasn't, too much — a good sport, a good man. He knew the same truths by heart.

I'd spent time in country I held dear — shared it with friends. That's all I could ask for. For me, the turkeys (I really mean this, Tim) are only an excuse to go out and play.

Most of my turkey hunting has been in the spring for a couple of reasons. The birds are much easier to get close to during this time of sexual arousal, and southeastern Montana is so far away, especially when you consider all of the great hunting and fishing within a four-hour radius of my home in Whitefish. There are browns running in the Clarks Fork, Huns on the Blackfeet Reservation, pheasants over by Bynum, rainbows in the Missouri, and so on. But one fall I did manage to make the trip, and it was not without incident, and that's par for the course when it comes to me and the big birds.

I had no plans, not the vaguest notion, to go chase the Merriam's until a derelict friend called from a bar in Busby. He was half blasted but I gathered that the birds were available.

"Holt, get your ass down here, the turkeys are on the move," and I could hear Tom T. Hall playing on the jukebox amid the background clutter of soggy conversation, clinking glasses, rattling ice, crashing pool balls, and general mayhem.

"I missed the first one. The sucker flew over the van and I shot out the windshield, missed the wife, though."

I learned that he'd been hunting in the general area of turkey camp, so I figured, "What the hell?" loaded up the truck with shotguns, flyrods (remember the browns of disbelief?), food, beverages, camping gear, and some cameras. Nothing major seemed in the offing.

That was a few days earlier. Now, only my death seemed imminent. The countryside had vanished in a hard-sided blizzard of wet snow. The truck was stalled in the gumbo mud and even with chains on the tires, I figured I was history. Yesterday had been warm for October, in the sixties; today was winter. Off the road translated into a long, long walk to the nearest house, maybe twelve miles if I made it that far. Freezing rock-hard seemed far more likely, well-preserved until next spring when I'd thaw and provide an April treat for the turkey vultures and the ants and the flies. Maybe I'd amount to something after all. Seriously, I was in some trouble at the moment. Relying on what has worked in the past, I climbed back in the truck, took a long pull on a half-full bottle of Jim Beam, and mulled things over. I remembered the friend who first brought me here. Where was he now?

This nameless friend, another good guy, called one fall and regaled me with tales of turkey hunting for more than an hour, saying things like, "You had to be there, John. [I'd heard this one before and it usually meant some kind of trouble.] I was sitting down in this big clump of bushes and turkeys were gobbling everywhere. I'd call and two of them answered and they kept getting closer. I didn't move and they kept coming in on each side of me. Their heads were stretching up and looking around and I'd hear *gobble, gobble, gobble.* It was great. I had to shoot out of self-defense. What could I do?

"So, John. Do you want to go next spring?" I said "Yes," even though I knew better. This was the guy who'd managed to con me into hunting sapphires and garnets on the Missouri River, moss agate in the middle of the Yellowstone River during spring runoff on a partially submerged gravel bar, brown trout on the Madison during a whiteout in October, and northern pike fishing on the Flathead River where our guides managed to get three trucks stuck in the river. So I went and we had a blast and I've been back at least once every year, both for the turkeys and the elusive browns.

I sat in my truck, reflecting on friends and turkeys as the snow was coming down. I was dead. Well, the wife and kids would have to live with the stigma of an outdoor writer-husband-father who had died in a freak snowstorm while turkey hunting. Life is tough.

Two days ago I'd spotted a flock of the birds running into the Ponderosa as I neared camp. I took a few minutes doing the usual camp setup routine and then struck off for the woods. The bunch looked to be around twenty-five turkeys averaging maybe twenty pounds. A quarter-ton of crazed, feathered madness. I hoped they wouldn't charge. The Savage was only good for two birds at best.

"How'd the fool die this time?" they'd ask.

"The clown got trampled to death by a flock of turkeys."

"You knew the boy would buy it in some weird way."

"Did he leave his family any money to live on?"

"He was a writer."

"So they're broke."

Dropping down into a timbered valley that drifted toward a small stock pond, I spotted the birds coming over the rise. If they kept on in their present course, they'd pass right in front of me. I sneaked behind a large tree and watched as they came silently in a bizarre phalanx, blue heads bobbing, plump bronze bodies swinging from side to side in an avian lope. They looked goofy as hell. A big tom led the way. I could see him clearly, and I raised the gun to my shoulder, resting the barrel against the far side of the tree trunk, waiting for the troops to come back into view. The birds loomed not twenty yards away, oblivious, an army of feral dead heads.

I drew a bead on the old male right at shoulder height and fired. The magnum-powered 2s rolled the bird over and he tumbled downhill. The others ran and then leaped into the air, flying quickly over the ridge. They were amazingly graceful and swift in flight. With my Beretta I could have had another, though this would have violated the law and I never question anything the Montana Department of Fish, Wildlife, and Parks says or does. They're gods in my eyes. Just look what they did for the fishing in my part of the state! They put mysis shrimp in Flathead Lake and in the process wiped out the kokanee salmon population of more than two million fish. They've hidden behind bureaucratic bullshit for years while the bull trout have dwindled to near-extinction levels, so how could I possibly question the one-bird limit? But once again I digress.

The tom was still kicking. I finished him off with a .22 in the head and grabbed the big bird, easily a twenty-plus pounder, and struggled back uphill, a bit of an effort with the added weight on my back. This shooting was easy, not like the few times I'd hunted the birds in northern Illinois; those guys were sharp and very skittish. I guess the same holds true down South, where more hunters call in each other than actually kill turkeys. Every year I read about guys shooting each other by mistake. Sounds like tough sport to me.

After taking some real fakey-looking, staged photographs, I field dressed the bird, saving the feathers and cooling the carcass in the chill air. I was still excited by the shooting and decided to walk around some more with my cedar box call and camera. There were fresh droppings and feathers everywhere.

Sitting on a rocky point overlooking miles of coulees and bluffs, I worked the call. *Screech, screech, screech.* Every few minutes I did this and was rewarded with the sound of distant gobblings, a wild, beautiful sound out here, producing the same feeling in me that howling wolves in the mountains north of my home or bugling elk do. The feeling runs electric right through my guts. I kept up the sporadic calling and the bird answered, but he was a long way off and moving no closer. Then below me I spotted the largest, whitest, fluffiest coyote I'd ever seen. Big. Well-groomed. He raced silently up to me, or rather the place of the turkey sounds (my callings). When he spotted the human, there was a discernible look of amazement and disbelief. I snapped a couple of quick photos (that turned out) and then the dog was gone, vanished like a classic illusion. It was like he was never there at all.

What a day! A turkey and then calling in a wild animal intent upon grabbing an easy meal. I returned to camp.

After dinner everything was silent in the darkness. No wind. Nothing. And gradually the countryside lit up in an instrument-panel-green glow. The trees, the truck, the rocks were all casting dark shadows. Overhead, in the direction of Billings, the sky blazed in sheet after undulating sheet and myriad waves of color — the northern lights. The display was so bright that I could read the writing on the band of my smoldering cigar. "Cohiba." And the show did not let up for more than an hour. I stared heavenward until my neck ached. Then they suddenly quit and the Milky Way came into view as a wide, bright-white band arcing across the sky.

Just another night in the West. I finally went to sleep. By daybreak I could see that heavy weather was coming in fast. Breaking camp and throwing the gear haphazardly into the cab and the back bed took less than fifteen minutes, but in that time, rain started, turning quickly to snow, and I was totally drenched and damn cold. My hands were bright red. I fired up the truck, wiped the condensation from the windshield, and headed out.

As soon as I hit the dirt road, I knew I was in big trouble. The word "fucked," while objectionable to many, applied right now. The truck wanted to lurch and slide into the nearest ditch. The snow was now a blinding, hypnotic blizzard, and there were already a couple of inches of the crud on the ground. The wind raced sibilantly through the sagebrush. The top inch of dust and dirt on the road had turned into wet paste that slid like oil across the dry ground below. I made one slight rise, slid down the other side, and then came to a halt.

And that's where I am now. In the cab, sipping Beam and wondering what to do. I am cold and wet. The grass and sage near the truck are covered in white. The rest of the world is a void off over there somewhere.

I knew the weather would only get worse and some clown on the radio confirmed this assessment with a cutsey, humorous reading of a forecast that called for lots and lots of snow in the "southeastern corner of the state down along the Wyoming border. You all better head inside now, ya hear? Get along little dogies."

If I got out of this alive, this bozo was a dead man. I'd hunt him down and drop him with the magnum copper-plated 2s and no jury in the land would convict me, especially once my attorney played a tape of the guy's show. This moron made Howard Stern sound coherent.

I took one more blast of Beam and decided to go for it. Drive like hell until I crashed, went off the road, stalled, or made it out to the highway. Visions, in black-and-white, of Robert Mitchum in *Thunder Road*, danced luridly before my eyes.

Backing very slowly down and then as far up the back rise as possible was tense work. Looking ahead, I figured my best bet was straight-on at full speed and then a slight angling across the road to the right, cutting down on the pitch; that side looked rockier, offering more traction. I eased out the clutch and built up my speed, past forty-five, twisting and turning the wheel like a madman. In a quick glance in the rearview mirror, I saw a spray of mud and rock rooster-tailing in a long plume. This was the *big time* now. I'd either make this rise and the relatively smooth sailing up on the plateau, or I'd die trying. I did not want to — could not — walk a dozen miles in this weather. The truck slid and swerved like a lunatic luna moth homing in on the night light of its dreams. I smelled clutch. I never let off the gas as I went from second to third and back to second then quickly to third and once more into second and I flew over the crest sliding sideways, almost hitting piled rock on the left than careening to the right and a small ditch and then back and forth, back and forth, and I knew I'd made it (I still get jazzed to this day thinking about that rocket ride, like right now when I'm writing about all this).

In what seemed like a century but was less than thirty minutes, I was back on good road and headed for Ashland, where I stopped at The Office (my first time) and downed two boilermakers and walked back out to the truck. The poor rig was covered in a dense coat of red-brown mud all the way up to the passenger windows. I knocked some of the slop off with an ice-scraper, got in, and headed down the road to a warm motel room.

Nothing to this turkey hunting, man. You just get out there and go like hell as long as you can, and I'm still looking for that idiot disk jockey.

Chapter Seven

Spruce Grouse

"Let's do it now. Right here."

"What the hell are you talking about, Amy?"

"Don't play dumb. Let's screw, in the grass down there."

It was a warm September day, even up in these mountains west of Missoula, and we were young and in love, so we did it, right there, and then I went over and picked up the brace of spruce grouse that I'd doubled on twenty-five minutes earlier (remember, I was younger back then).

They were dark-feathered with bright marks the color of fresh blood above their eyes. There was blood, now almost dry, along their necks and flanks. I'd hit both in almost the same spot, one leaping up right after the other, easy shooting. Amy, who had never seen anything killed, yelled, "All right!" and her face was flushed red-pink and her grey-blue eyes were sparkling. I could tell she got off on the rush that is shooting. She was wired.

Amy finished pulling on her jeans and buttoning her plaid shirt. We walked down through thick forest to the Landcruiser, where we popped a bottle of Mumm's, ate some venison, Bermuda onion, homemade mayonnaise, and mustard on freshly baked, whole wheat bread sandwiches. We had another bottle of wine and smoked a joint — youthful freaksters enjoying an easy life in the early seventies. A good time, full of impulse and oh, so little responsibility.

This was the first time I'd taken Amy hunting. I'd met her while staying at the Holiday Inn in Missoula. My stepbrother and I were building a home in this drainage we were hunting today and

were holing up at the Inn until the walls and roof were completed. Amy was a barmaid at the Inn. A group named Lynn and Patty Jean provided the nighttime background music and we all became friends. The duo shared the room next to mine. After their last set, drinks were in order.

Amy was in her twenties with long blonde hair and a demon of a personality. You had to watch yourself or you'd get hurt. Within a few days, she started staying with me in my room and the management fired her. We said, "That's a shame," and it was a fun fall that lasted for several more contentious, wild years. Then we blew apart, in a hurry, just like those first two grouse blew up out of the ground cover in front of us.

My life is like that, though not as much as before. Good things never last as long as I'd like them to, and I have to believe that's my fault. A hard, egocentric son-of-a-bitch to live with.

But, needless to say, we went spruce grouse hunting a lot that year, and everytime I killed a bird, Amy wanted to make love right where I'd fired the shot. It was weird, but I got into the ritual, and I shot better that fall than I ever have before or since.

I know this seems a bit strange, perhaps flat-out weird, and it probably *is* twisted, but I remember one day we were culminating the spruce grouse shooting in this special way when Amy said, while we were embracing, "Shoot the gun, now. Right here."

So I grabbed the over-under Browning, and Amy held me up with her hands on my chest and I fired, twice, and her nails scratched me, and I can truthfully say I've never made love like that in my life, not before or after.

So that was how my spruce grouse hunting went more than twenty years ago. It was exciting work; you never knew what would happen. I still love to shoot the spruce, but today's outings are more sedate and that's okay. Those memories are plenty, and I'm married to a woman who is tougher, more honest and loving, a better friend than Amy ever thought of being and that's perfect, as it should be.

Spruce grouse are the archetypical fool hen, a bird seemingly without brains. The species displays such stupidity, a complete lack of fear at the sight of hunters, that trying to make these birds fly can be almost impossible. There have been times when I've thrown rocks at the grouse while a companion waited for the things to take to the air. Sometimes they never did, and there were outings when the creatures would not even walk, let alone run, away. I hit one with a palm-sized chunk of rock in the wing some years back. This broke the bird's wing, forcing us to shoot the bird in the head. Wonderful sport. The grouse's mates just stood around watching the show. We retrieved the bird and drove off in search of better action, any action.

At other times the spruce grouse will fly to a tree limb, and stand motionless, convinced it is invisible. Usually, it will then absolutely refuse to fly. Sticks, rocks, shots above its head — all are useless. At times, the grouse really deserve the derogatory nickname.

According to a number of books I've read, the ruffed grouse is supposed to average a little bit larger than the spruce grouse. The reverse seems to be true where I've hunted the birds in the northwest corner of Montana. The spruce run around sixteen to eighteen inches, the ruffed just a bit less.

Spruce grouse males have black breasts with white spotting along the sides. The tail is black with some more white spotting at either side of its base. Some of the birds shade toward brown, similar in appearance to females, though this is not common in the northern Rockies. The females sport well-barred plumage and a chestnut-colored tail. Males have a telltale red comb above the eye.

They are by nature solitary birds, and I've rarely kicked up more than four or five at a time. The norm is one or two. At the risk of anthropomorphizing, maybe somewhere deep in their pea brains, spruce grouse realize they really don't have much to say to each other. I doubt this is remotely true, but the birds do not seem gregarious as a species in my experience.

In the mountains running north and south near my home, the most productive habitat seems to be in lodgepole pine tree and huckleberry country, especially if there are seeps or small creeks trickling away in the area. You have to develop "spruce grouse eyes" when they are holding in this deep cover that is often gloomy even at midday. The birds' dark coloring makes them nearly invisible. When they do their statue act, they basically vanish. Any dog is a plus at these times, with scent being the only clue to their presence. There are spots that I know hold the grouse consistently, so I have faith that I'll find birds. This seems to increase my concentration, and I'll run across several in an afternoon.

Basically, the behavior of spruce grouse is pellucid in nature. Find country that is not heavily hunted (local populations can be decimated by even a few hunters working an area thoroughly for several straight days), in lodgepole pine with abundant food such as pine needles and wild berries, add a little water, and there will be grouse.

A general rule for me is that spruce grouse prefer lower elevations and thicker cover than ruffs, who like Douglas fir and wet meadows, country that is usually a little higher above sea level. The blue grouse like the wide-open, sheer drops of the windy ridges.

As for eating, I've found that some spruce grouse are a bit strong in taste, especially older birds that have lived almost exclusively on pine needles. The flavor is distinctive and the meat stringy. Soaking the dark-meated birds in milk or salted water seems to help. Sautéing the birds in butter and white wine, allowing the meat to cool, and then adding it to a stew of onions, carrots, potatoes, chanterelle mushrooms, and a gravy made with a roux of flour and butter makes for a hot supper around a campfire. Season the mixture with freshly ground sea salt and white pepper.

Sourdough bread and some Burgundy completes an acceptable repast.

Younger birds that appear to have been feeding more heavily on huckleberries and maybe rosehips (check the crops) are always excellent breasted-out, rubbed with a little oil, seasoned with salt and pepper, and cooked over very hot coals. The oil will flare and seal in the juices. Once again, a little sourdough bread with unsalted butter and some full-bodied red (or white if that's all there is lying around) wine makes for a pleasant dinner around the fire as night sneaks up in the mountains. As long as there is plenty of what's being cooked, the simpler the menu, the better when hiding out in the hills.

There are times when I've shot birds up in blue grouse country, on the open ridges above most of the trees. One bald summit, again west of Missoula, was the site of an abandoned fire lookout. The road up used to be sporting as it wound through thick pines and then along a very narrow, rocky cut on the side of the mountain. Going up, the passenger had an excellent view of dropoffs ranging up to several hundred feet. The road was somewhere under the rig, out of sight. I preferred driving.

Just before the final switchbacks to the structure, we would park the Landcruiser and walk through the trees. We often shot the spruce and some blues when we jumped them along the road, quick flights requiring quicker shooting before the birds disappeared over the ridge, flying like the wind down to dense timber.

Walking up the lane the last few hundred yards, we'd often spy spruce grouse in the grass or taking grit in the road. They were slower on the uptake than ruffed grouse or sharptails, but as soon as they realized that the two creatures coming toward them were not illusions of trees waving back and forth in the distance, they hopped up and were immediately on their way, always right over the ridge.

One time there were a couple of grouse and they hit the air, then dropped right over the side of the road. I fired twice, drawing feathers and dusting the ground. I ran to the edge and the grouse were already tiny specks darting toward a timbered swale far below. Ejecting the empties and loading two more shells, I launched the loads out over the void for the hell of it. The sound of the shots died quickly in the wind.

Coming around the last turn, I saw two more grouse plucking at tall grass growing around the support posts of the lookout. By the time the gun was shoulder-high, the spruce grouse were starting to fly. I doubled on both of them with the first shot. They rose one behind the other. I fired the second load, too eager to control my reactions, and splattered dark brown splinters of road into the air. One of the grouse was still alive, flapping its wings pathetically. I wrung its neck and threw it and its buddy into the game pouch of my vest.

My friend was an old cruising buddy from years gone by, and we weren't hunting hard; I had to be content with the shooting and a nip from a flask. This was fine. The view from the encircling porch of the lookout was magnificent. Ridge after ridge of mountains rolling away into the Selway-Bitterroot Wilderness and eastern Idaho. Missoula was barely visible in the east, and the Flathead Valley and its many mountain ranges rose in the north. The view lasted forever, and then we finally noticed that the sun was closing in on the horizon.

Walking back to the rig, we jumped two singles that my friend nailed easily, being a natural and graceful shooter. Four grouse that we took back to the Holiday Inn (the home was not completed yet) and asked the cook to prepare for us, which he did. Perfectly broiled birds sitting on mounds of wild rice and accompanied with broccoli buried in Hollandaise. We felt like kings, and made a grand show of enjoying our meal. Minds of children on parade in public. Lynn and Patty Jean could be heard warming up in the dark lounge behind us. Showtime.

I n western Montana, very few folks hunt mountain grouse. In fact. I know only a few people who do. That's fine, actually great. The less pressure, the more birds and the less the chance of running into other hunters when I'm walking my favorite covers in the Whitefish, Salish, and Swan mountains.

Finding spruce grouse is not difficult. Usually I spend many hours bouncing to and from high country streams and lakes from late spring through the bird season. I spot the birds all the time, and I make quick notes about when and where I found the grouse. Sometimes I pull over and try to find more grouse, walking far into the woods beneath tall fir or edging between lodgepole pine packed so tightly together that I'm sure there is no way a deer or elk (or grizzly) could squeeze through.

In the lighter areas, huckleberries cover the ground, some of the bushes reaching as high as my waist. In July and August when I'm out scouting around, a lot of time is spent picking the fruit. In good years, the berries are as big around as a marble and tartly sweet. Within minutes my fingers are stained dark purple and juice runs down my chin. A class act. I can tell by the droppings beneath the plants that grouse and other animals like this food as well.

Narrow game trails track through the ground cover, winding around impassable stands of pine and over graying deadfalls that are worn down from the passing of many feet. In the afternoon of a sunny day, even in thick forest, the air grows hot. Flies and mosquitoes swirl in the dead air, attacking my face and arms, taking chunks of meat from my balding scalp, and trying to fly up my nose. I hate these bugs, but they are part of the grand scheme of things up here, though I've never caught a trout on a deer fly, never seen one in its stomach when I've cleaned fish for a late supper or big breakfast. Their usefulness evades me.

The mosquitoes drive me nuts with their high-pitched whining. There is nothing worse than being cooped up in a claustrophobic tent trying to sleep through a steady rain, and one damn mosquito takes it upon himself to create an insect version of hell. I've ripped tent walls and hit myself in the head in the dark, yet never managed to kill that dreaded "lone mosquito." The bites don't bother me much. I've been bitten so many times, my system has acquired some sort of immunity. It's the solitary whirring of those wings that makes me crazy. Perhaps I'll bomb the tent with Raid the next time.

By the first of September I've checked most of my older covers, discovered some new spots, and have a fair idea of where to go hunting for the spruce, ruffed, and blue grouse in northwest Montana. I've also managed to pin down the locations of some pheasants. If I had the time to hunt whitetail and mule deer along with elk, I'd know where to work for these animals, too.

I'm not a whiz at locating these things, but finding game is as much a function of keeping my eyes open and investing a lot of hours in the woods as anything. As an old friend who taught me the ropes of the aluminum siding sales game always said,"Even a blind squirrel can find a nut."

There is a series of boggy meadows that used to be lakes filled with small (and some large) brook trout now long gone. I hunt this land somewhat regularly. Working along overgrown logging roads that border the openings can be interesting shooting if the spruce grouse let you approach close enough and then once you do, decide to fly. The shots are quick because the birds vanish quickly through the willowy brush and around behind the fir, spruce, and lodgepole.

On a wet September morning I walked along these byways, already covered with a damp carpet of leaves. The pines were dark green, dripping minute droplets of moisture they'd collected from the damp atmosphere. The sky was low, the clouds swirling not far above the trees. The mountains were cut off at the knees in the thick banks of weather. The place was spooky. The hair on my neck prickled. I kept looking over my shoulder. Maybe a grizzly was in the area, or maybe some crazed psychopathic serial killer recently escaped from Deer Lodge State Prison. I didn't know, but the woods were resonating eerie vibes. I pushed on, aiming for the meadows. I'd break out in the open and walk back to the truck away from the forest in the safety of the light.

As I crossed a small creek, I wondered if there were any trout finning away in the pools and below the miniature waterfalls. While staring into the water, I was startled by crashing and stomping and loud snorting not far to my left, in thick cover.

"Oh shit!"and I tried to run toward a large pine. I hoped to climb the tree before I was run over by the crazed beast that I was certain wanted to take my name out of the phone book. I never made the tree. I tripped over a deadfall partially buried in the ground and fell head first into a patch of spongy, soaking moss. The gun slid off a bush and landed next to the stream. Fortunately, the safety held or things could have been even more exciting. My knee was in rough shape, the ligaments stretched farther than they were meant to be, and the pain was like someone chiseling out the cartilage of the mangled joint with a dull, rusty screwdriver.

And then I saw the moose, huge as it towered above me, its long, fleshy bell swinging darkly as it hammered through undercover I could only crawl beneath on a good day.

I was sure I was dead, about to be stomped to bloody mush beneath those pounding hooves. Bigger than anything alive I'd ever crossed in this country, the moose freight-trained right by me, rocking the ground with a vibration I could feel in my guts. Huge. Terrifying. And then the animal was gone. I could hear it splashing through the nearby meadow, the sounds of sucking mud as it pulled through the marsh came squishing through the air and, thank God, diminishing in volume.

That's as close as I've ever come to being killed by a wild animal. I've jumped bears, but they've, fortunately, always moved off in the opposite direction, human scent translating in a bear's mind to trouble or death or something sickly alien. But this moose was *pissed*. I'd startled it during breakfast, and I don't know why it did not beat the stuffing out of me. Standing up slowly, I felt the damaged ligaments throbbing, doing their wobbly best to hold the knee together. The gun was wet and had two new scratches near the trigger guard. If I live to be eight-hundred, I'll never forget how they got there. The abandoned logging road was the only way back. The wounded joint would never make it through the sucking meadow.

I gimped my way gingerly toward the truck, scared as hell, adrenaline making my face and arms glow and feel radiant. Only a little farther. I could make out small flashes of the tan body of the pickup. I thought the moose was back. Then I simultaneously fell to the ground on my bad knee and raised the shotgun. The pain didn't hurt, it burned, and all I could think was, "This is it, you son-of-a-bitch. You're going to have to shoot and you're not going to win this one," as two damn spruce grouse blasted right across my face, only feet away, and I sank into the wet road. They were gone before the shooting reflex surfaced. Heart pounding. I'd had enough. The knee, originally wrecked playing football as a kid (yes, a real football knee) would have to be fixed this winter (that was last year and I still haven't gotten around to the surgery. This winter for sure).

I made it to the truck. Unloaded the gun. Took a leak. Lit a cigar and drank a cup of coffee.

Christ! That was easily the most exciting grouse hunt I'd ever been on, and I never shot a bird. I decided to back off on the shooting for a few days. Give the woods and my weird, but good luck a chance to recharge.

My son Jack is almost to the age where the idea of hunting is more than some vague notion involving mystery and intrigue, so I decided to take him with me to the mountains north of town in search of spruce grouse. My children have been a gift, a way of seeing the world through clear eyes. This outing was no different.

We slowly negotiated the washed-out road, plowing through deep puddles of muddy water and over rocky gullies before we turned up an old skid trail. We got out and I grabbed the Savage .22/20-gauge. Light rain was falling and the forest was cloaked in patches of fog that hung like shrouds around the dark trees. Once again there was an other-worldly feeling in the woods, though Jack's enthusiasm and constant questions weakened the intensity of the sensation.

"Have you fished that stream, Dad?" Jack asked as he slid down a leaf-covered bank to the edge of the water. "Are there fish here?"

The creek was two feet wide and maybe a foot deep at the most, but I noticed dark shapes race for the cover of an undercut bank.

"Just saw some small cutthroat, but I've never fished here. Too small and too many overhanging limbs." We moved on up the trail, gaining altitude quickly. I was panting a bit, but Jack was moving easily with the energy of youth. We began crossing patches of snow and I saw grouse tracks, which I pointed out.

"They're the same shape as *Tyrannosaurus Rex*, but a lot smaller," my son observed, and that triggered a spirited discussion on the evolutionary relationship between birds and dinosaurs. We walked some more without seeing a grouse or anything else alive. There were lots of small deer tracks, some old grouse sign, and claw marks on a large lodgepole that indicated a black bear had visited the area sometime this year. The sap was still running and the wounds were bright, so we talked about bears, mostly grizzlies, for some distance.

We dropped down a hill into a stand of large Ponderosa. Squirrels ratcheted away at us from the limbs above as they bombed us with pine cones.

"Can we shoot those?"

"No. Too small and I never shoot anything I'm not going to eat."

"Why not?"

"Never waste anything wild," was all I could think of, but added, "After you've killed a bird, we'll talk about it again."

And we walked some more and still didn't see any grouse, but Jack was totally immersed in the forest, picking up the pine cones and throwing them in the air, examining rocks and mushrooms and finding some empty shells from somebody else's hunt.

We stopped at a downed pine and sat down and shared a candy bar. Jack asked if he could fire the gun. I unloaded the shotshell, set the selector for the .22 barrel, positioned the gun in his arms, butt tight to his shoulder. He'd never fired a gun of any kind before (he was only seven), and he pulled the trigger. The shot echoed through the damp woods and he turned to me with a look of wonder and excitement that I doubt had crossed my face in a decade. The joy of being a kid. The whole planet is something new and different.

"That was neat, Dad!" and I basked in unaccustomed paternal euphoria. It was time to start showing my son the beginnings of the world I lived for. I had to slow down on the trips and the writing for a living (money, that is earning the stuff, is a drag). We spent time going over safety with a weapon — how to carry a gun, when to load and unload it, how to push the safety, never shooting at anything until you were dead sure it was what you were seeking (horror stories of morons shooting at moving tree limbs thinking they were deer horns only to discover they'd killed a human ran through my head). And we shot up a box of .22s, blasting a stump at the base of the hill, before we retraced our steps back to the truck.

We shared a thermos of hot chocolate and another candy bar before heading home. A most satisfying day, and the following year I made a point of taking each of my children — Jack, Elizabeth, and Rachel — on individual trips to favorite trout waters. Rachel loves to fish, once hanging on for dear life to a flyrod I'd handed her that was bent sharply to the weight of a big lake trout. I suddenly realized the fish was pulling her toward the current, and I grabbed the rod, landing the fish, which she proudly held aloft, shining and sparkling in the early morning light. But she said,"You caught this. It's yours."

Hunting and fishing with fine friends is what being in good country is all about. But, like I said, my children are a gift.

When I think about, consider all the experiences, I am forced to admit that for a"dumb"species, spruce grouse have given me some of the most intense, unique hunting experiences.

Not far from where I crossed tracks with the marauding moose, I was working a relatively open patch of woods. The ground was huckleberry bush and moss and wild rose, and the pines had wide trunks that towered above for more than a hundred feet. There was a small, lazy creek that meandered through another meadow that was once a series of lakes now diminished to ponds.

A huge heron lifted off from a rotting log, moving silently and majestically into the air. Until the wings moved, I never had an inkling that the bird was there, standing stick-like next to the water. I watched as the heron disappeared over a copse of aspen. Brook trout were rising to small caddis flies. I could see the dark blues of their backs, the blaze oranges of their bellies, and the white tipping of their fins as they rose in graceful arcs while feeding on the bugs. The lake was a riot of concentric feeding circles. I wished for my two-weight flyrod, but pushed on through the trees.

As I came into a clearing, a single spruce grouse jumped up, headed for the safety of a large limb. He never made it — a brain-dead simple shot at the dark bird as he rose almost straight in the air. He hit the soft ground in a muffled thump, feathers gliding slowly down in short back-and-forth swings and landing on his lifeless body. There was blood, a bright crimson drop, in the crease of his beak. The fluid matched the color of the combs over his eyes. The forest was silent again. The acrid tang of gunpowder was thick. I love that smell.

I walked on. Always walking. Bird hunting and walking. As I came over a slight rise, a bunch of spruce grouse leaped into the air, headed once again up and for the limbs. I fired and two birds fell, and I fired again and a single collapsed. I was stunned. A triple? Not for this boy, but it was true and it is the only one I've ever turned. I felt like Elmer Keith. The game pouch was heavy with the weight of the four grouse as I headed back to the old road and the waiting truck. (I've spent so many miles, so much time in that pickup, that the rig seems like a dependable friend, always there.)

The wild, colorful brook trout were still rising. The sky was clearing off, hints of light blue peaking through the fast-moving clouds. The air smelled of the pines and the marsh, of autumn. I kept walking.

Fool Hens, maybe, but fine, good-crazy times with the spruce grouse. I enjoy everything about these birds. Tomorrow I'd bring the flyrod along, too.

Chapter Eight

Blue Grouse

The white antenna dishes flared across the flat top of the mountain above. Control stations with globe roofs looking like giant puffball mushrooms were clustered beneath the antennas, and radio towers rose hundreds of feet higher still. This was a military and commercial relay station complex that controlled much of the airwave traffic for the region. The place looked abandoned, empty of humans, but I knew there were a few hunkered down over glowing, technicolored instrument panels in otherwise dark rooms. A strange place to hunt blue grouse, but the birds were here, scattered among the pines that grew on all but that uppermost barren stand of man-made confusion.

I worked through the trees on the edge of a rocky ridge. Miles and miles of timbered mountains stretched off to the West in corrugated consistency. Large clearcuts dotted the scene. In the east, the tallest peaks of the Swan Range seemed immense even at a distance of many miles. Farther away, the white summits of Glacier Park shredded the sky with jagged vehemence.

Radar stations and the northern Rockies, coexisting up here in contradictory juxtaposition. Where in the hell was the West heading? I sure didn't know.

Walking some more, I angled closer to the edge, and the grouse blew up in a noisy flapping of wings and boisterous squawkings. I fired out of shocked reaction, hitting the trailing bird of the bunch with the second shot, rolling it over the side of the mountain. This would be fun. I *loved* creeping and scrambling along a sheer slope with rotten, fractured rock sliding away beneath me.

I found the grouse piled up in a jumble of boulders, an avian crash without survivors. Setting the gun down in some bear-grass, I scrambled down and retrieved the bird, medium gray on the breast like a chukar and substantially larger than either a ruffed or spruce grouse. Bright yellow combs streaked over the eyes. The large fan-like tail was set off by a much lighter band spanning the feather tips. White on the throat. I'd hit the grouse hard and most of the right wing and flank were blistered in ragged fashion, feathers missing.

After walking through this series of covers, basically one square mile of habitat, my feet were sore from negotiating downfalls and small, jagged rocks. I'd killed two other blues right off the bat, near the truck. Enough for one day. I found the wide gravel road and started walking back when more birds busted from the matted ground cover, and I hit the lead one as it crossed the road twenty yards ahead. I know — absolutely *know* —I could have dropped the other, but the limit was four, so I swung through the grouse and passed on the shot.

I rarely shoot well enough to take a limit, even when the birds are all over the place like today, a cloudy, windy October morning. And taking a limit is never that important. Being outside by myself way up here with this outrageous view is plenty. If I have a few opportunities to shoot and make a racket and even nail a blue or two, I'm satisfied to some extent most of the time — an easy mark in my own right. Some days, everything clicks and the shooting is second nature, instinctive. On blues flying like maniacs with the wind, zeroed in on cresting the nearest ridge, they are tough targets. A limit is rare. The accuracy juice doesn't flow often, but when it does, it sure is sweet.

As with the ruffed and the spruce, it seems that very few people hunt mountain grouse in northwest Montana or anywhere else in big-game country in the West. I've never seen another bird hunter up this way; maybe somebody glassing the hills for deer, or late-season mushroom pickers, or perhaps a couple of aging hipsters smoking the day away on the hood of a road-weary Ford Torino — stuff like that.

Why so few people hunt upland birds here is a mystery. True, stalking and then killing a big animal is thrilling, skillful work,

but so is kicking up the grouse and then trying to raise the gun, factor in the rapidly shifting variables, and then making (or missing) the shot. It all happens so fast, I'm amazed when I do as well as I've done today. One or two blues can be chalked up to random luck (any luck is appreciated, random included). A limit on difficult shots means some level of nascent skill has surfaced, if only for an instant.

Back at the truck, I drop the grouse in the crusty snow in the bed of the pickup. On days I get a few birds, I feel like a hunter, more than some clown who misses a lot and covers the disappointment with catchy jive, like, "Just being out is enough," and, "What a day to be alive." I've said all of this many times and meant it, but the days are a whole bunch better when I have some birds to clean and some decent shots to remember.

The blues have already cooled and they sink only slightly in the snow as the last of their body heat dissipates. I pull off the boots, a wonderful feeling, like shedding a heavy backpack after a long, uphill death march. I pull on a dry pair of socks (my feet were sweaty in the insulated uplanders) and a pair of whisper-soft leather moccasins. I pour a cup of very strong black coffee and add a splash of bourbon out of a skinny silver flask from the glove box. There is a strong, cheap Bering cigar hiding in among shotgun shells, flashlights, maps, and a space blanket. It lights in a small explosion of sparks and hissing founts of blue smoke. Smells awful, tastes great. It goes well with the drink that steams around my face as I sip it. The hot liquid slides to my stomach where it burns with fine heat.

I never hunt blues until October. I like to walk the wide-open ridges in the morning as the wind cuts through me. The days are measurably shorter now. The dim sun never climbs as high in the sky as I want it to. The nearness of a long, cold season triggers an intensity that compliments chasing the blues, or perhaps its the other way around. It doesn't matter; these grouse symbolize the almost frenetic need I have to squeeze a few more days out of a dying year. From the looks of things, this fall may already be DOA.

Some nasty weather is on the loose. I can see black, roiling clouds pouring over the mountains in Glacier. When storms come in from the northeast, trouble in the form of wind, heavy snow, and extreme cold is not far behind. When a system powers over the Continental Divide with enough energy to look like a dark night descending on the valley at midday, it's time to get off this mountain and race home for cover and warmth. October is too early for such nonsense, but winter comes when it feels like it around here. I was planning to head over those obscured mountains in a few days to chase some big brown trout and hunt up some pheasants, but that may be a dead issue. The way the storm is closing in, I may have a tussle reaching the safety of lower ground.

The truck fires right up as always, and the weather report on the local AM radio station calls for a winter storm warning, meaning the roads will be impassable by four a.m. and the mercury will be hanging out with the twenty-below crowd. Oh well. I'd do some writing until things moderated a bit. I make the valley floor as the snow starts drifting down. By the time I clear Kalispell thirty minutes later, the snow is slanting down in dizzying curtains and blowing in skiffs across the pavement. Twenty minutes later when I pull into the front yard, the ground is covered and the larches are swaying at dangerous angles, the wind roaring through their tops. The last of the fading yellow pine needles mix with the snow, creating a bright blizzard. Safe at home by an inch.

Blue grouse and open ridges are a single image, but early in the season the birds are often hundreds of feet lower than they were on this hunt. Unlike other grouse, the blues move up higher as the weather grows colder. Most singles I've encountered have been males. Lower down, the ratio leans in favor of hens and birds of the year. The males apparently move downslope to meet the females halfway and consummate their breeding. The young are normally raised in lower country during the spring and summer.

The grouse likes berries, including the ubiquitous huckleberry along with snowberry and bearberry. They also eat plants like clover, and insects that include grasshoppers and crickets, with a preference for the former. In a warm autumn, working clearing edges is about the only time I've shot the species in the open away from timbered ridges. Blue grouse are not as quick on the launch as ruffs, unless they take off downhill where they present difficult targets.

Subspecies include sooty and dusky grouse. The dusky is found in the Rockies, and the sooty variety lives in the mountains of the Pacific coast. Also, like the ruffed and the spruce, they have a strong tendency to fly to the nearest limb and hold still, almost impossible to pick out among the branches, thick clumps of needles, and dark tangles of moss. The birds are often found in small groups, but they never seem to form large coveys like sharptails. In the first snows, they are easy to track as they wander among the trees in search of food. Once flushed and shot over, they are next to impossible to follow up. They will fly more than a mile downridge at these times. A retriever is an excellent aid for locating downed birds that have fallen in among the broken rock and springy ground cover.

I always use my Beretta 20-gauge. It's a light, graceful little gun that was a gift from my stepfather. We always hunted and fished a good deal together during each trip he made to Montana in the fall, except this last one when Goddamned cancer took him away. I hate that disease with a passion.

In Michael McIntosh's *Best Guns*, he has this to say about Berettas, "...The rest of the world shoots more Berettas than anything else. The reason is simple: Beretta builds a superb gun from a deep understanding of what a gun ought to be, a commitment to building it that way, and from having been around long enough to figure how to do it."

Or as Steve Smith told me "If they made fewer of those guns, they would be worth at least $3,000."

That's good enough for me, but the main reasons I love the little gun is that it feels perfect in my hands, shoots were I swing it, and it reminds me of my stepfather. That's what counts.

One outing, I'd pulled over alongside a logging road, the highways of the woods, to show him some particularly impressive clearcuts. Large, open expanses of barren ground rolled off as far as we could see. Work to be proud of. Denuded mountains dominated the skyline. I had the gun out for the hell of it, as we walked down the road for another vantage point, a second chance to savor the woodland carnage. A blue as big as a sage grouse (it seemed that way at first sight) streaked from the slope above us and arrowed straight for the tall timber below. I brought the gun up, locked on the grouse, swung through, and rolled him into the trees. I was pleased — decent shot in front of a relative. A vast improvement over the days when I used to call him from college begging for money. I was sure he would be impressed.

"Nice shot, John," he said and added, "You plan on crawling down there after him?"

"Sure," and then I looked over the edge of the road into the most jumbled pile of downed slash I'd ever seen. The bird was just beyond this mess lying in some beargrass, but I wasn't sure if I could get to it. The slash looked like a giant pick-up-sticks game designed by a madman. I'd never been here before.

"See you later. I'll watch from here," my father said. So I handed him the gun and started risking my life to retrieve the blue and save face.

I slipped and dropped through the tangle, twisting my ankles and knees and breaking the skin on the tops of my hands. My palms were scraped bloody from sharp protrusions of splintered pine. I got to the bird and then repeated the painful process in reverse. I was sweating heavily, bleeding some, and wiped out, but I had the bird. My father was sitting on the tailgate sipping a beer.

"I can see why you like to hunt grouse up here," and he belched with admirable resonance. "You make the whole game look like fun."

I thought about asking him for some more money, but passed on the idea and opened a beer instead. I'm sure he was impressed. Fathers, especially good-friend stepfathers, are tough. He finished his beer, climbed in the truck, and said, "Move it, John. It's time to go."

Of such joys are fond memories made.

I've had a recurring dream about blue grouse, the only time I ever dream about birds unless you count the one I frequently have where all magazine editors look like Pterydactls that are diving like a squadron of Messerschmidt 109s straight down from an awful yellow sky, intent upon ripping my bloody fingers from my hands. Actually I'm no longer sure any more if this one is really a dream. Recent experiences lead me to believe otherwise. Sure, I know the ones about owning twelve-cylinder Jaguars and having even a few bucks in the bank or walking around downtown Whitefish without any pants on are genuine fantasies (at least I hope so regarding the last one), but this number...I'm not so sure. At any rate, the dream about the blue grouse was just as surreal as the one involving the editors, but in a pleasant sort of way.

I was far up on a ridge in the Whitefish Range working north toward British Columbia. I could see the wide clearcut band running up and down the timbered mountains, east to west, the actual physical line that marked the border between Canada and the U.S. just like on a paper map, and I remember thinking, "Stupid bastards." A small stream was sparkling over a creekbed of brightly colored rocks. The rushing water sounded like suspended diamonds brushing together in a soothing breeze. Huge — six feet or more — bull trout were arcing far out over the water in pursuit of mayflies with wingspans like that of vampire bats. When the char crashed back into the water, the sound was like shattering mirrors.

Farther upstream, a grizzly sow of fifteen feet or so and weighing many tons was teaching her yearling cubs how to catch the bull trout. She would bat the fish out of the stream and fling them against massive larch trees with trunks as big around as farm silos. When the fish smacked against the trees, a wave of sound like someone throwing a brick into a harp rushed over me. The cubs preferred splashing in the stream and playing hide-and-seek in the timber. Mother was not pleased and howled like a Kansas tornado. The kids returned to their lessons.

I looked up and admired the pink midday sky. I was carrying the Beretta and a small pack filled with whiskey, matches, seasonings, butter, a space blanket, some nesting pots, a ten-weight travel rod and reel, a box of flies, and some cigars. I had a knife in a sheath on my belt. I was set. Trees on a far ridge climbed five-hundred feet into the sky, their glowing emerald needles refracting the gold light in strange directions.

I knew this was a dream, and not to be taken seriously, but the landscape seemed so familiar. I didn't care if I ever woke up. I was comfortable in this place.

I worked up a steep slope of scree, sliding in the loose, iron-gray rock. Sapphires and garnets were lying among the stones, the gems as big as billiard balls. I loaded several in the pack. On top of this new ridge I pushed through huckleberry bushes bearing fruit the size of baseballs. And then three blue grouse burst up in front of me, larger than ostriches. Their beating wings sounded like helicopters. I shot twice and dropped the lead bird with a nice passing shot as the trio streaked over the ridge, headed the way I had just come. The big bird rolled all the way down the slope, landing near where I planned to set up camp. A perfect shot.

I could still see the bull trout rising as I trotted downhill. The landscape was bathed in an orange-gold haze. The sky was now the color of well-oxygenated blood. I couldn't wait to clean the grouse and to cast huge streamers to the fish. What would six-foot bull trout weigh? Two hundred pounds? I never found out. Instead, I woke up. A big disappointment. I looked at the bedside clock. Three a.m. A bad time. A time for the screaming terrors of consciousness. What am I doing here? Who am I, really? Is any of this worth the effort? How in the hell am I going to pay the bills?

The dream sequence was still fresh in my mind, still real. I wrote it down in a small note pad and tried to turn off the lunatic blues. It was futile, so I got up, made coffee, and read a book. I think it was *Blood Root* by Thomas Mordaine, and I thought my dream was way out there.

So much for sanity.

When I learned of my stepfather's death in October, I thought I had things together — under control. We'd said our goodbyes last summer at the traditional family vacation spot on the north shore of Lake Huron in Ontario. I was wrong. Ken's death affected me deeply. I had trouble talking with my family and friends. I couldn't work. I didn't give a damn about the bills. None of any of it seemed important. I was lucky I didn't land in jail, though I wouldn't have cared at the time.

Rather than work, I spent the days hunting and fishing where he and I spent time together; at night I got drunk. This went on until one day Lynda pulled me back with an angry outburst of some duration about love and responsibility. It was work that needed to be done — on both our parts.

But while I was in my mood, one of the places I revisited was back up in the Whitefish Range not far from a couple of turquoise lakes and a beautiful little stream that holds a population of native west slope cutthroat trout. There are elk, wolverines, deer, grizzlies, sometimes mountain caribou, spruce grouse, eagles, ravens, biting insects, raw mountain ranges, thick virgin forests, very few people, and superb blue grouse habitat. In short, my kind of country. And Ken's, too.

One spaced-out, clear, perfect blue-sky September a few seasons ago, we had worked along one of the more accessible ridges, kicking up blues every so often and hitting a bird once in awhile. The view of this wild country was staggering. Miles and miles of unspoiled landscape in every direction, and Ken and I looked at each and laughed. There was nothing to say. Back at the truck, sitting on the tailgate drinking ice-cold Beck's Ale, we didn't say much then, either. Words were worthless, excess baggage, on this outing.

The grouse were piled between us, already field-dressed. The grays, blacks, whites, and comb yellows of the plumage were intense in the sharp sunlight. A nice sight. I put my hand on top of that mound of blues and marveled at the feathery smooth softness, a nice sensation. That's how that day felt, and I'm glad I have this memory, but it hurts hard to think about it, and it hurts a lot worse to know I won't be hunting with Ken in country that sweet on days like that ever again. Some things aren't right.

There is another pocket of wildness in those same mountains that feels like home. If there are things like reincarnation (and I think it's basically a mind trick to avoid dealing with this life), well then, I've been here many times in the past, the distant past.

Tucked way back in the heart of grizzly country is a landscape of deep green fir giving way to scrub alpine firs on the exposed granite ridgetops. Small sapphire lakes tinged with glacial flour (powdered rock ground from heavy accumulations of snow and ice) lie in tiny alluvial basins. The walk in is a long one, more than a dozen miles, much of it climbing steeply. The trail is one made by the deer and other animals (I never use the word "critter." Beware of anyone who does. Don't take my word for this. Find out on your own. Just a little advice.). The path is mostly overgrown with berry bushes and tag alder as it nears the small creeks that tumble out of the highlands.

There is always fresh bear sign, or "steamers" as my cousin likes to call them, along the way. Ravens croak overhead. In the fall, elk can be heard bugling among the peaks. I first came here because of rumors of large, wild cutthroat trout. The fish were in the lakes, all right, and larger than I'd been told. This alone was sufficient reason to keep coming back. But on the way I flushed plenty of spruce grouse, and I pushed up blues in astounding number along the windy slopes in amongst the scraggly timber.

I don't know why this habitat produces so many of the grouse, but they are everywhere in singles, doubles, and squads of a half-dozen or more. The walking is difficult. I use hiking boots instead of my bird-hunting pair; the stiffness is needed to handle the sharp, loose rock. It seems that I am always sidehilling when the grouse burst from the battered, twisted pines. If I'm below the grouse when they flush, they fly down over me anyway, rather than upslope into the wind.

Maintaining footing and balance while swinging on the blues as they whip by is entertaining, a precarious proposition. I've passed on shots for fear of falling and rolling a long, rocky way down the mountain. When I've hit the birds, it's been when I've swung well past and below them in an attempt to gauge where they'll be when the shot arrives. I'm usually well off the mark, but the few hits are rewarding. The bird will collapse into a ball, still moving forward with the momentum of flight, then tumble into the slate-gray rock, sliding hundreds of feet toward the lakes below. The feathers scatter swiftly in the wind. Retrieving is a bitch, but worth the effort because of the vantage point during the shooting. Seeing the hit blues fall far out of the sky while watching from above is like flying. The action is all below me, not quite in real time. A strange sensation that almost draws me off the side of the mountain, then I catch myself and lean back in toward hard ground and reality. Too bad. Maybe I should leap after the falling grouse one time. You never know.

On one saddle in these mountains, the wind seems to blast up both sides of the ridge. Standing on the edge of the defile trying not to yield to acrophobic terror while being buffeted by the raging atmosphere is a free-form ride of the wildest, puissant dimensions. I feel like a minor god screaming at the world below. Wonderful therapy that accomplishes nothing. I'm still just as nuts as always, but at least I'm captain of my own ship on this saddle. The peaks of Glacier wail away in the east, and the timbered hills that are the Salish Mountains glide far to the west, as pretty a place as I've ever been. But real gods only let pretend gods fake it for so long and I realize this, so I drop back down to the lakes, picking up two blues I'd shot earlier along the way.

The cooked flesh tastes of the wind and ice and the weather-blasted pines. I do nothing to them after they are cleaned but cook them plain over a bed of glowing-red coals. The meat is not juicy but is delicious, tasting a little of blood. Two birds fill me. The fire leaps at me when I toss the carcasses and a couple small limbs on the coals. I light one of the last of my Havanas and inhale the rich, chocolate-tasting smoke. A sip of Glenfiddich works well. Only the best in this country. Only the best.

The ridge where I stood earlier in the day playing the part of the lonely madman railing away blindly at life is silhouetted against a shining silver blaze cast by the setting sun. I work on the cigar and the Scotch and listen to the forest turn on for the night. Animal sounds and ghostly whisperings through the pines. The wind? Unknown spirits? Contemporary music with ancient rhythms.

I look back up to the ridge, now almost one with the dark sky, and think about the blue grouse holding tight in the austere cover. That's all. Nothing profound. I just wonder how they're doing on that steep edge of oblivion.

Chapter Nine

Pheasant

Colors exploded as the birds rioted out of this northwest
Montana wheat field. The pheasants were making a break for
it. Crimsons, emeralds, red-browns, tans, blacks, buffs, silvers,
blues, golds, turquoises, and of course the white rings around the
necks. Cocks, hens, and young of the year; it was out of control.
Metallic-sounding squawkings shattered the silence. Alert the
community. A dozen birds, maybe more, were on the loose, coming
out of the tan wheat now bone dry and almost waist-high.

My friend and I both fired. I saw two cocks drop back into
the grain. He'd doubled. I caught up with one of the leading birds,
slapped the trigger, and rolled him into the grass growing alongside the gravel road. I swung on another, an easy rising shot, and
missed. By the time we had reloaded, the pheasants were all spread
out, hiding in another wheat field across the road. My friend's yellow Lab made the three tough retrieves in routine fashion, as slick
and graceful as a 4-6-3 double-play in baseball.

The honey-colored hound was muscular yet lithe with a
handsome head, a classic specimen of his proud breed. He was
well-trained, intelligent, strong, and heavily imbued with that best
of all Labrador genetic traits: the willingness, indeed, the overriding
need, to please people, especially his master (I hate this term, but I
can't come up with anything that works as well).

These birds were heavy; no, make that plump bordering on
fat. The grain crop had been outstanding and the year mild, and
wet at the right times. There were healthy populations of pheasants
throughout the state. These three cocks averaged a little less than
thirty inches in length and had extremely long tails. More excellent

feathers for both of our fly-tying benches. We shoved the pheasants in our game pouches and walked across the road. The afternoon was warm for late September, in the upper seventies, maybe playing with the low eighties. I wore a t-shirt and a mesh vest. This truly was one of those days when it was good to be alive.

The Lab soon turned birdy, tail wagging in a frenzied circle, shoulders cocked and head tight to the ground. He swiftly flushed a quartet of hens that kept flying until they were out of sight. Then a cock jumped up only a few yards ahead, too close to shoot unless I wanted pre-made pheasant burgers. I followed him until he doubled his distance from me and then dropped him in a cloud of feathers, the bird moving forward a foot or two and then falling in a heap. The Lab brought this one to me. Unlike many retrievers that only bring downed game to their owners (is *this* a better word?), he could figure out who shot what and make the fetch accordingly.

Then three cocks hit the air in an evenly spaced line twenty yards away, spooky birds sharing scary vibes. I hit one on the right and my friend dropped the middle one. We were done, and even if the limit had been higher, we would not have shot any more cocks out of these fields. There were a lot of pheasants in the area, but neither one of us likes to shoot specific groups down to next to nothing. Perhaps this didn't enter the population equation for this species, but why mess with a smooth-running system?

Biologists have told me that it is probably better to shoot all of the cocks out of any given area, that even when the males appear to be all gone, eliminated by hunting, predators, and disease, there are still perhaps as many as one cock for every six hens, more than enough. The biologists say the older males eat more than their share of grain, depriving the younger birds of valuable nutrition and, in turn, hunters of a bumper crop of birds next fall. Whatever. We're stubborn and will do things our own way.

Hunting pheasants in western Montana seems anomalous for someone who was raised in the Midwest, a land where a hill of over 600 feet often boasts a ski slope. Walking back to our car, I looked east out over the fields to several ranges of mountains towering above the valley. Fresh snow, already a couple of feet deep, extended down well below treeline into the timber. In a few weeks, the white stuff would complete the downward journey, covering the last two thousand feet in a series of fast-moving storms that would steadily grow in intensity. Autumn is the best time by far in the West, but the season never lasts long enough, and winter is like a dead-broke house guest who has cleaned out the liquor cabinet and plans on staying another week. The sucker just won't leave.

Putting aside this ugliness, I must say that, like most upland shooters, I love to hunt pheasants as much as any game bird. I like to hunt them as much as chukar (probably more as I grow older), Huns, mountain grouse, and even sharps. Actually, it seems my favorite bird is the one I'm currently hunting, just like my favorite trout species is the one I'm casting over at the moment. Pheasants were the first game birds I ever shot many years ago in southern Wisconsin. I still remember the surprise and the elation when a fast-flying bird actually fell to the ground because of my shooting. It was like rare magic (and on bad days, still seems like rare magic).

The Eurasian transplant is found all over Montana, especially where there are grain fields, thick cover along creeks and drainage ditches, or hay fields. Like the other Western upland birds, pheasants are ground-nesters, but they will roost in larger bushes and in trees. In the best cover, a dog is mandatory or there won't be any shooting. There is no way a human can work acres and acres of agrarian land or force his way through thick cane that looks like prime holding country for a Cape buffalo. Two dogs who work well together are even better, with two or three gunners walking the line and another one or two serving as blockers. This drives the pheasants, squeezing the birds together toward the blockers, forcing them up within easy range. Blockers are a hardy breed, based on the few times I've done this chore, shot raining down on me from the heavens. No thanks. I'll pass.

Whether in Wisconsin, South Dakota, or Montana, the birds tend to feed both in the middle of the morning and the middle of the afternoon, watering around noon. Often when they're feeding they flush wild, then again, in thick cover like a Midwestern soybean field, you need a dog that crawls on his knees to kick up the birds, but more on that phenomenon later.

Pheasants also seem to prefer the edges bordering most structures like drainage ditches, marshes, creeks, and rivers. In cold weather the birds will often be holding down in these corridors, almost impossible to flush. They sit tight and cast a weak scent. It's tough, slow work requiring patience and thoroughness, two of my finer qualities. I usually look for food, shelter, and water when hunting unfamiliar territory known to hold the birds, grain fields, hayfields, and water of some sort a basic combination. The best fields are those that have seen little machinery activity or livestock grazing. And no cover is too thick for the birds, which run like marathoners at times. There have been days when I've been unable to locate the birds, but not many. In this respect I've been fortunate concerning pheasants.

I'd never seen a dog crawl on its belly trying to kick up pheasants, nor any other game bird, but that is what was going on today. The Big Tall Dummy's dog, an Irish setter by breed, a full-blown ball of nervous energy by nature, was pushing his way through a stretch of some of the thickest cover I'd ever encountered. All I could see of Rusty was his wagging tail and his hind legs extended out behind him pushing frantically into the ground-level unknown.

As mentioned earlier in the book, no one would ever accuse Rusty or the two of us of being disciplined, accomplished hunters. We were out for a good time, and if that included shooting a few birds, well, that was okay.

We'd both done a lot of hunting back in Wisconsin, where my friend still went to college, eight years and counting, but a Bachelor's degree now seemed like more than a poorly defined goal. Maybe another two years would see him through. He was out staying with me in Missoula, and neither of us was attending classes with any consistency. He claimed to be doing off-campus work study. Apparently this included lots of beer, awfully late nights, and loads of fishing and hunting. Who cared? We were having fun; it was the early seventies and we didn't know any better.

We were stumbling around on some rancher's land a long way from Opheim, a small community of well under two hundred. Opheim itself was a long way from anywhere, the nearest town of substance being Glasgow, fifty miles to the south. Again, who cared? We'd stumbled on this location while hunting Huns earlier on another ranch lying well to the west. Driving down the beat-up road, we saw cock pheasants flying in front of us, standing next to the road, and strutting along the edges of fields. We figured this would be easy pickings and we might have been right, but it seemed a bit early to tell.

We opened and closed a number of barbed-wire gates on the way in. I actually found myself standing on the proper side of each closure instead of watching my friend pull away in the truck while I stood with my hands on the wire looking like a World War II prisoner. Gates and I don't get along all that well. We were headed to a series of grain fields separated by rough drainages carved by spring floods and intermittent stream flows. The rancher here knew the rancher who had let us hunt Huns, and it turned out that they were friends. He invited us into his house, stepped into the kitchen, and made a phone call to check out our credibility. Possibly a problem? Apparently we passed the test, because he drew a map on a piece of notebook paper and said there were more pheasants "out there than I can ever remember."

This was big, open, huge country. Larger than anything we had hunted in Wisconsin. The land rolled away in all directions. There were no county or state roads anywhere. If we looked at a good map of where we thought we were, all we would see would be an irregularly shaped rectangle covering 1,500 square miles of creek bottoms, hills, and a bluff here and there. Roads that were impassable much of the year outlined the parcel. Elevation ranged from about 2,000 feet in the drainages to maybe 3,500 feet up top. All of this land drained into the Milk River flowing turbidly somewhere down south of us. Where the Milk now sprawls through a wide, spacious valley, the Missouri once ran. This area is now filled with glacial debris from the last ice age 15,000 years ago. The Milk owns the land in a free-form way now.

The country was brown, nothing was growing, the land-scape waiting until spring warmth and infrequent rains turned things green again. This was early November and it was barely above thirty degrees. The sky was a thick mat of gray clouds. The wind was blowing as it always does out here, and I was feeling a little overwhelmed, intimidated, by all of this openness. My friend never worried about such things, about much of anything at all. He was driving with one hand while twisting and turning our original map with the other as he tried to guide us to an old windmill and a stock tank, major landmarks out this way. There was supposed to be a small wooden shed nearby, too.

After an hour I was ready to give up. I used to be that way all the time, but over the years I've gotten to the state of mind where I don't care where I am as long as I can at least maintain the illusion of purpose. It no longer takes much to turn this easy trick. The thought of these pheasants will work every time now that I'm in my forties.

As I said, I was ready to give up, to head back to Opheim and then down to Glasgow for some drinks and a warm motel room, but my friend said to hold on, we were almost there. He was right. Cresting a hill that gave way to acres of flat fields, we spied the windmill a mile away. As we neared, we could see that it was rusted, crooked, and bent. Pulling up by the tank and getting out, we looked for the shed. It was right on the other side of the tank, collapsed into a heap of gray, rotting boards and timber. I won-dered when was the last time the rancher had been to this spot. The blade of the windmill spun erratically in the wind, making a nerve-tingling, screeching sound.

We headed out to the fields, working along the edges just above a cut in the land that was full almost to the top with weeds, brush, bushes, and some sort of deranged trees. No way could a person cross that stuff, but that is where Rusty was working now.

Earlier in the season, we had to let him run for an hour or more, kicking up birds miles away, far out of range. Eventually he would tire and turn into a help rather than a source of maddening frustration. This far into the fall, the dog had learned more than either of us. He loved to flush birds. I think he enjoyed the sound of our shooting, and he did a pretty fair job of retrieving. True, some of the birds, two sharptails in particular, came back slightly chewed around the edges and coated with Irish setter saliva, but we all have our shortcomings.

The Dummy whispered (he never whispered), "Holt, heads up. The dog's going to get us some birds any second now."

I was ready, gun almost to my shoulder. Rusty was lost from view, out of sight, but I could hear him digging away in the tangled crud, and sometimes the top layer of this desiccated growth shook a bit with the dog's efforts.

And then we heard the pheasants make that alarmed sound that reminds me of a piece of cord being pulled in short strips through a hole in a tin can. Next, we saw a pair of cocks, brightly colored and looking big, explode through the cover. Rusty was right behind as he tried to snare them in his jaws, but the brush held him back, and he collapsed on top of it with his front legs coming to rest on the plants. We could see his head, shoulders, and legs; not his hindquarters, though. He looked like he was resting on a ratty couch.

We both fired at once, my friend three times with his pump and me twice with an over-under, and both birds dropped into the overgrown ditch. Rusty was gone now looking for the dead birds.

"Holt, we'll never see those pheasants."

"Hell, Jon, we'll be lucky if we ever see your dog again."

Minutes passed and we each smoked a Camel straight. We could hear the dog rooting around below us somewhere out of sight.

"Rusty. Rusty, come here, Goddammit," my friend yelled, but still no setter.

More time passed and then the brush parted and Rusty staggered out with a pheasant, dropped it at my feet, and was gone again.

"Holt, what the hell have you done to my dog? You've been giving him Jim Beam again, haven't you?"

"No, Jon. I don't do those things. He brought me the bird I shot. Maybe you missed yours."

"Bullshit," he huffed and we killed a few more minutes with another brace of Camels. Then there was a tremendous racket. We could hear brush being kicked around, limbs breaking, and a couple of excited barks from Rusty. I worried about the possibility of a badger, but kept this thought to myself. And, miraculously, it seems so to me to this day, Rusty appeared with another pheasant that he deposited at Jon's feet. I'd never seen anything like it, and I still haven't.

"Do you believe this shit, Holt?"

I didn't, but that was as dedicated a piece of work by a dog I've ever experienced.

"We're not going to improve on this. Let's head back for a beer at that joint back in town."

I was ready. One of the few things we'd learned during the course of several mistake-ridden years together raising hell all over kingdom-come was not to press our luck.

We started walking back and Rusty flushed several hens. Almost to the truck, the dog turned another pair of roosters and we both made a lot of noise launching five shells. Amazingly, both birds crumpled. Rusty brought them both back with direct, crisp retrieves.

"Holt. Something's wrong here. We never had a day where things went so well."

We'd shot a lot of pheasants together, but my friend was correct. We'd never had a day go quite this smoothly amidst the potential for things to go very wrong.

"Let's get out of here while we can," I yelled as we started to load up. I had visions of lightning strikes, an Indian attack, or four flats on the truck. But we'd played our cards right, maybe a bit conservatively. We even found town and the bar and a cheap room and lived through the night to go hunting the next day. We weren't about to complain.

Much of the upland bird hunting I and many others do is solitary in nature. We enjoy the chance to spend time alone or with one or two close friends and our dogs, walking through fields and woodlots, lost in our own thoughts. Mountain grouse and chukar hunting come to mind in this respect.

Pheasant hunting can be like this, but it is also one of the birds that attracts a celebratory atmosphere of fellowship and good times. Something like a marginally disciplined Chinese fire drill. Seven, eight, or more hunters can work fields for the birds with impunity. One group can drive the pheasants from the far end of a large cover while the others wait with intense eagerness for the flushed pheasants to fly their way. Then the roles are reversed, and so on throughout the day. One such example of this occurred during a November hunt in central Montana.

I'd known Chuck and Blanche Johnson for a few years, back from the days when they were selling sporting books through the mail while living in Ohio. I knew Ohio. My first wife came from Parma outside of Cleveland, and the few good times I'd had over there were at Municipal Stadium at night watching the Indians lose to somebody. Anybody. Everybody. I'd be drinking cans of Stroh's beer as I took in the action up in the free-oxygen seats of the upper deck. Good times. Anyway, I was glad Chuck and Blanche had moved their business and their lives to Montana, to Bozeman.

Over the past year, we'd fished and hunted some together and talked over the phone a lot. They spent a few days at our place in June, and the four of us got along well. They liked Lynda and she liked them.

Now Lynda and I were headed over to central Montana to do some mid-November pheasant hunting. Steve Bodio and his friend Libby Frishman would be there and so would Steve Smith, the poor soul who had to edit this book.

I'd known Bodio for a long time, though we never met until we attended a conference last August at Big Sky. Prior to that, he did his best at getting my work published in *Gray's Sporting Journal*, actually succeeding once with an off-the-wall piece about hundreds of grizzly bears, Kessler's whiskey, and Glacier Park. When we finally met, it was like we'd been friends for many years. We drank a lot of whiskey together in those three days. The Bodio-Holt Rule came into existence on that trip. After 10 p.m., only one bottle of whiskey apiece for those two clowns.

Libby was at Big Sky, and I liked her immediately. Chuck and Blanche were at that conference, too, and the operative phrase during our stay was, "Party in Room 137." We had a fine time, even coming up with a variation on the old tele-evangelist scam. This one was based on the sacred concept of aluminum siding and the right for all free men to sell the product in any state, in any small town, they so desired. It was fundamentalism in a hustler's sort of way, and I think it would work, but the person we ordained as the Reverend Dig Deep (another conference attendee) has been seen only infrequently around Montana. I've heard he's hustling a book on the environment. We plan a conclave for next spring. We want our cut from the Reverend; he knows this, and I think he may be on the duck. We'll see.

As we raced down through a small valley and then up on the Great Plains, I thought about how nice it would be to see these people, my friends, again. I didn't know about this Steve Smith character. We'd never met, but I wasn't worried. We had guns and two kegs of ale donated once again by my friend, the owner of the Whitefish Brewery. And as I said before, Lynda was tough.

We found the house that Chuck and Blanche had rented and before I could draw a beer, Chuck and Steve Smith came out the front door. Oh Jesus, Smith (Smitty) was wearing a dapper hat, a waxed-cotton coat, Wellingtons, and was smoking a pipe. *I'm through*, I thought, but we hit off immediately, and then Libby and Steve pulled in with a springer spaniel answering to the name of Bart. I'd brought over a 16-gauge Darne for Bodio. I'd played a sort of middleman along with Chuck on the deal, and in no time both Bodio and Smith had gun cases open on the frozen ground, comparing guns.

Eventually we made it to the ranch we were to hunt. We were shown around the land, told where the birds were, and what draws to avoid; another group was going to chase whitetails toward sundown in one or two of them. Lynda and I walked one side of a brushy creek, sticking to the high ground. Chuck and Chris Francis (manager of habitat for Ted Turner's little place in the Gallatin River country) worked the lower marshy ground with one of Chuck's German wirehairs. Within minutes they flushed pheasants and dropped one apiece. Lynda and I watched from a superior vantage point, seeing the birds drop almost before we heard the shooting.

Minutes later I heard a yell, turned in time to see a cock flying high and 100 yards away. I fired, knowing I'd never hit the bird. At that range you could have caught the spent shot with a basket, but I wanted to hear the report and feel the slight kick. I was happy. Chuck, as is his custom, managed to break through thin ice (the only kind he knows) and get chillingly wet. All in an afternoon's work. Smith had also broken through and, being experienced in such matters, had pilfered the last dry pair of socks from Chuck's truck, a slick little back-East move.

That's how the day went, and when we all hooked up to hunt some pockets of brush and some sere grass hills, the sun was heading home and clouds were sliding in. The air was cold and the snow crunched like rotten Styrofoam. Smitty had lost his pipe while shooting a Hun that ran away probably never to be retrieved. While we all looked for the pipe, Chuck's dog found the wounded Hun, snatching the cripple as it vainly tried to take flight. This was a quarter-mile from where it had been shot initially.

We walked some more behind Chuck's dogs, dear sweet Annie was out now, too. And Bart was happily engaged in the hunt. We all talked about shooting and other things and Lynda commented, "Seven adults out walking the dogs," and we laughed. That, in a way, sums up bird hunting and probably said more about this passion of ours than she had intended.

Bart's ears were packed with burrs, so while Bodio attended to the problem we ended our hunt with large glasses of Black Bart Ale. Things were cold out now, and it was nice to reach town and the house that already felt a bit like home with all the friends around.

Bodio had cleaned a pheasant he'd taken (on a high crossing shot) in the kitchen sink, and the gut pile cast a curious aroma, one that gagged Lynda some. She remedied this by building a drink dominated by Tangueray gin. I made Bodio and myself some Jack Daniels over ice, and everybody else fended for themselves. The Bodio-Holt rules, by mutual consent, had been suspended for this occasion.

How to explain conversation and drinks and good food and late nights far from home — the things that are so much a part of upland bird hunting, any hunting or fishing? Lynda and Smitty hit it off and talked on and on, and Chuck, Steve, and Blanche were laughing about something, and Libby was telling me about climbing sheer rock walls. It all made a convoluted type of sense. I don't think any world problems have ever been solved during these joyous sessions, and I'm not all that sure that all that much is remembered or worth remembering, but it is this fellowship as much as any other aspect of life well spent outdoors that draws me back over and over again to good country, rough weather, and fine sport. It is one more chance to share time with dear friends. How many of these do I have left? It's all pretty simple, but I live for these things.

The next day broke cold and a storm was moving in from the northwest, powering down along the Rocky Mountain Front from Canada. We worked along the creek again, but turned only a lone sharptail. Moving across the highway, we worked a narrow valley lined with old pines and filled with marsh and cattails. My bad knee had given out earlier, so Lynda and I took the easy route along open ground. Below us, above an old, earthen dam, the others got into a bunch of pheasants, dropping the colorful roosters with regularity. The dogs had a field day and the shooting was sporting.

Pheasants began to flush immediately from the brush and cattails below. Apparently the birds had been driven, had escaped the previous hunting pressure, from the creek across the highway. They all seemed to be over here.

Smith was working along the edge of the dam well ahead of us when a cockbird broke up the steep face of the impoundment then broke sharply away toward distant fields at the sight of a hunter. What looked like a difficult shot was rendered gracefully easy (only in watching). The pheasant never had a chance as Smith rolled it with an excellent shot as the bird tried to dive for safety beneath him. Duke proceeded to point at least fifteen, probably close to twenty, pheasants in the ensuing forty-five minutes of spirited action.

In one sequence, Duke went on point near Bodio, who yelled, "Chuck, there's no bird down here," and Chuck said, "You're right on top of it. He's holding at Duke's nose." The pheasant broke, its long tail feathers brushing Bodio's face. Close, startling work.

And then another bird flushed nearby with Bodio hitting it first and then Chuck finishing it off before it had a chance to fly off into thick, wet cover. And that's how things went, with Duke going on point time after time, Chick limiting out in what he termed "one of the best days I've had. I've never shot better." And the others all took pheasants in the darkening, chilling day. Fine sport in a dandy little piece of habitat. What pheasant hunting, all upland hunting is about — lots of action providing a variety of challenging shots..

But then we saw Bodio hurrying up to the dam where we stood. He was carrying Bart. The poor dog's eyes were glazed. He was drooling, and his hind legs wouldn't work. Libby rushed to get the car while we wondered if he'd eaten some poisoned predator bait. Concern dropped down on us like the storm now boiling above. Steve and Libby raced Bart to town in search of a vet; we decided to hunt a little more. What else could we do?

No more birds, and on the way down Lynda and I trailed behind the other three. We talked about this and that. With three children, our times alone together are limited. Closing in on the trio, Lynda turned and whispered to me, "I didn't know Chuck used two hearing-aids. This caught me by surprise and I looked discreetly at Chuck's ears. There *were* two orange plastic objects in them.

"They're earplugs, Lynda," and I couldn't help laughing, and she did too, after a pause. The others cracked up when I relayed the comment, and another long-lived anecdote was born. Now whenever she answers the phone and Chuck or Smitty is on the end of the line, they shout, "*Lynda. Can you hear me? Is John around?.*" Earplugs and hearing-aids. And so it goes.

When we returned to the house, Bodio was there and looked relieved, informing us that the cold and the hard work and Bart's age all conspired to knock him down with hypoglycemia, which we had suspected. The prognosis was good, and Bart was at the vet's receiving a sucrose boost. Bart would spend the night there as a precaution. Relieved, we lounged around watching parts of the Montana-Montana State and the Florida State-Notre Dame games. The Grizzlies and the Irish won.

Chuck, Blanche, Smitty, and myself went back out to the hunting grounds and worked steadily up and down drainages with no luck. The weather was cold and the birds were holding tight. We pushed through the creek drainage one more time as the afternoon darkened and the snow set in. No luck and time for home, where we found Bodio in a state of high anxiety. He'd lost his wallet, but we located it at the bottom of the leather gun case that held the Darne. Put a bunch of writers, editors, publishers, and their patient women together, and organized mayhem becomes a natural adjunct of day-to-day activity.

We were all wind-burned and glowing from the warmth of the home. Cocktail hour. Bodio and I signed books for each other and for Smitty. While some of us showered — we were due at the home of Don Thomas (another writer) for dinner in an hour or so — I mentioned to Chuck that I was putting together a trip for 1995 to chase taimen. These are huge salmonids (members of the trout clan) that reach weights exceeding two hundred pounds.

"I'll do the book, John," Chuck offered, and another crazed project was launched.

"Count me in,"said Bodio, and I knew there was no hope for some of us. Now it looked like Steve — and my friends Baton Rouge Kevin, Boston George, and Bob Jones — and myself would be lugging gear far into the Gobi Desert in search of the city of Abu Bataar and then onward and upward hunting the mysterious taimen.

Bird hunting often leads to these things.

Don Thomas lived on a hillside above a wonderful spring creek. I'd packed a travel rod, but it was snowing like crazy, so I passed. Plus it was pitch dark. Don was generous, filling us with good red wine, wild game, and interesting conversation about his part of the world. The night wound on and Dire Straits was playing in the background.

Sounds like pheasant hunting to me.

Then we were back at the rented home talking over whiskey about writing. A sad situation to be sure, but an unavoidable deal. I held forth with the righteous indignation of a free-lancer, moaning about how we never get paid on time or enough, but nobody really paid attention or cared, as it should be. Just talk.

The last morning Lynda and I headed back. We passed on one more hunt. We parted company secure in the knowledge that this gathering would be an annual affair. I noticed that Chuck had dropped two roosters in the back of the truck. A great guy. The roads were glare ice from last night's storm, and a trip that took six hours coming in would eventually require eight hours of white-knuckle, thirty-mile-an-hour driving through a wind-driven white-out along the Front.

So, no birds for me, but still one of the best times I've ever had chasing game birds or anything else for that matter. Lynda and I got to spend time together. She got to make new friends. I got to know Smitty and to spend time with people I really like. Some years back when my life was more than a little ugly way too often, a weekend like this one was beyond imagination, way out there laughing in the farther reaches of another star system.

All of this is by way of explaining that killing birds is only part of it. There's so much more. So *much more*. It all seems so simple and easy to me at the moment, but I know, just like when things are going good like on that long-ago hunt with the Big Tall Dummy, you never push too hard, and you never take anything for granted.

Epilogue

One last time this year. This would *have* to be the end of things. Winter arrived ahead of schedule, bringing along its delightful personality riddled with frigid temperatures, blowing snow, and too-short days.

I'd parked the truck several miles down below by a wooden bridge that crosses a clear stream now almost covered with ice. In the middle, where the water runs the deepest and swiftest, dark ribbons of current move sluggishly, as thick as blood. Where I am now, high up along an exposed ridge, the life is gone, leaving only broken seams of exposed rock. Not much else that I can see. Down below me the forest is no longer emerald; instead, the pines are shaded a blackish green that is all but extinguished by the thick covering of powdery snow.

Why I am up here is an easy one: Bird season flies by too quickly, in an instant, and I wanted to be out in this country one last time before everything locked up, before the roads and trails, the woods themselves, are sealed under many feet of snow.

Earlier this summer, on a warm, shining afternoon, I'd wandered the ridge among the dwarf alpine firs. Wearing only jeans, a cotton shirt, and tennis shoes, I was perfectly comfortable. I was scouting out the country, looking for grouse, but they were down playing in the pines. Hell, all I was really up for was to look out over everything. To be alone. The mountains rising above looked benign, even friendly, though I knew they could kill me in an instant of inattention or plain old random bad luck. That's a chance always worth the taking. Better to die up here in a rock slide than down in a filthy city from a case of virulent mundaneness.

Even this late in the season there are blue grouse around. I see tracks and droppings around the wells of barren ground beneath the gnarled stumps.

This year I'd been able to get out for days that added up to weeks. The birds had been out here, though some species were on their down-cycle as far as populations go. I'd been fortunate enough to shoot at least one of each of the nine upland species, and that was a first, something I'd try to repeat next year.

For now, I wanted one more bird to end the year.

Walking along in the cold wind, I thought about all of the fine country I'd hunted and all of the friends I'd spent time with. Never enough, but even a taste of something good is better than nothing at all. There would be next season and many more after that, I hope. Walking the dry rocks of the badlands looking for crazy chukars. Tramping through thick forest seeking mountain grouse. Wandering the high plains chasing sharptails. Stumbling about in the sage flats tracking sage grouse.

As in fishing, I've spent enough time in this country, even learned a few things, to begin to have a sense of the seasonal rhythms. There are times when certain species will be in specific places, and I know a bit more in this respect — only a little, but it all adds up after awhile. The more I sense these cycles and changes, the faster time seems to move. I find myself spending large chunks of time outside and it still is never enough. Years are starting to slide past at a terrifying pace.

Looking back on this season, when I think of all the hunting and walking, this all appears to be a lengthy process. Standing on this mountain, I don't think so. The first of September was yesterday or maybe this morning. How did October disappear so fast? and what about November? That's the way the years are moving now, too.

Where is all this madness heading? I used to ask myself. I don't care any more. I don't give a damn. It's not important, and I'm powerless to change the direction of events that are my life. Too much philosophizing is dangerous for some of us. I'd rather be like the birds, taking on the passing seconds one at a time, each a perfect moment. I'll find out soon enough where all of this winds up. Thinking too much only rushes the process, and I'm in no hurry. None whatsoever.

My feet are cold. I'm cold. Time to head back down the slope to the truck and some coffee and a cigar. No grouse today. All of a sudden it's like the theory of the last cast. When you think the fishing is done for the day, you make that one last cast, and a big brown trout hammers the bedraggled fly. Why this happens so often, I'll never know. Do we radiate some intensity that alerts the game when we're keyed into our passions?

A blue grouse explodes from beneath a ragged fir tree. Snow trails behind like a vapor trail. I bring the gun up without thinking. Instinctively. I pick up the bird flying like crazy for the forest way down there. Swinging through and beneath the fast-moving blue, I pull the trigger....

Notes & Comments

Ninety percent of my upland bird hunting takes place in Montana. I have plenty of chances to travel to places in the Midwest or in New England or in states like Wyoming and Idaho, or even to Mexico or Canada and so on, but I hate to leave my home at any time, autumn in particular. There are just too many things going on: Upland birds are everywhere and big browns, brookies, and rainbows are on the move. The countryside is turning on color-wise. Some of the best weather of the year shows up. So why leave? If you want to find out for yourself, the following information will be helpful to you in planning a hunt in this state.

For those who have never hunted birds in Montana or have no one to refer them to an honest guide or outfitter, call the Montana Travel Department and request the travel package that includes pamphlets (more like magazines) on recreation, food and lodging, fishing, and things to do along with a road map. The recreation guide is a gold mine, even for longtime state residents. Information on all licensed guides and outfitters (if you're a bad operator or dishonest in Montana, you don't stay licensed for long) is included along with contact numbers for agencies like Fish, Wildlife and Parks, the Forest Service, and many state and local chambers of commerce and travel agencies. There is also a listing of public and private campgrounds. All of this may be obtained by writing: Travel Montana, Department of Commerce, Helena, MT 59620; or by calling (800) 541-1447 outside of the state or 444-2654 in-state.

Maps are favorite toys of mine. Some of the best include one of Montana (other states are also available) that is a 40 x 60-inch relief map that costs twenty-five dollars and is worth the price. Two other maps that are glove box size and very accurate (far better than the state's road map) are the Recreation Map of East Montana and its western counterpart. Other states are also available. These are the best maps of their kind I've found anywhere and well worth the three bucks apiece they cost. These may be obtained from: Western GeoGraphics, Box 1984, Canon City, CO 81215; (719) 275-8948.

What clothing and guns to bring is subjective to a large extent. Just remember that it can be summer hot or winter cold in September and October and very cold in November. Bring rain gear, good boots, and layered clothing.

Upland bird hunting, and hunting in general, has a long history as far as the written word goes. Quality writing abounds. The following lengthy list includes some of the best writing, a bit of nepotism, and some self-promotion.

A Breed Apart: *A Tribute to the Sporting Dogs that Own Our Souls*: a collection of essays that include works by George Bird Evans, Geoffry Norman, Charles Fergus, Robert F. Jones, and many others..

Dreaming The Lion: Reflections on Hunting, Fishing, and a Search for the Wild by Thomas McIntyre: A couple dozen essays on everything from hunting lions to chasing down dinosaurs.

Blood Ties: *Nature, Culture, and the Hunt* by Ted Kerasote: A thoughtful, well-reasoned exploration of why we hunt and a subtle rebuttal to anti-hunters everywhere.

Bare November Days *A Tribute to Ruffed Grouse, King of Upland Birds*: an anthology on the pursuit including works by Gene Hill, Michael McIntosh, Tom Huggler, and others.

The Orvis Book of Upland Bird Shooting by Geoffrey Norman: An excellent entry-level book to the sport.

The Diamond Bogo by Robert F. Jones: Easily the most unique novel on hunting around.

A Field Guide to Mammal Tracking in North America by James Halfpenny: A good book on this segment of woodcraft. Sometimes it's nice to know what you're about to get into or what's been following you along the winding trail.

Blood Meridian or the Evening Redness in the West by Cormac McCarthy: One of the toughest novels ever written, this one about the ultimate game animal, hunted relentlessly in the harshest of environments.

Harper & Row's Complete Field Guide to North American Wildlife assembled by James Ellison: The best of this type of guide on the market.

Hunting Upland Birds by Charles F. Waterman: An older book, but still one of the most informative penned by one of my favorite outdoor writers.

The Way Of The Hunter - The Art and the Spirit of Modern Hunting by Thomas McIntyre: To say that McIntyre is a talented writer is like saying he likes to hunt a bit.

The Hunter's Guide to Montana by Mark Henckel: The best book on this subject. Nothing else comes close.

Hunting the Great Plains by John Barsness: Some good writing here by a Montana native.

Drummer in the Woods by Burton Spiller: Stories about grouse hunting.

A Hunter's Road - A Journey with Gun and Dog Across the American Uplands by Jim Fergus: One of the finest books ever written on bird hunting.

<u>A Rough Shooting Dog: Reflections from Thick and Uncivil Sorts of Places</u> by Charles Fergus: A wonderful book about a bird hunter and his dog.

<u>The Upland Gunner's Book</u> by George Bird Evans: Required reading for all bird hunters.

<u>Pheasants of the Mind</u> by Datus Proper: Possibly the definitive title on the subject.

<u>Shotgunner's Notebook: The Advice and Reflections of a Wingshooter</u> by Gene Hill: A classic that discusses all aspects of bird hunting.

<u>Best Guns</u> by Michael McIntosh: A thorough, exhaustive treatment of the best shotguns ever made by one of the subject's leading authorities.

<u>A.H. Fox — The Finest Gun in the World</u> by Michael McIntosh: So well conceived and written, this book reads like a novel.

<u>Querencia</u> by Steve Bodio: As good a book as has been written by anyone in any genre in a hell of a long time. An emotional story of love and death and freedom that took guts to write.

<u>Good Guns</u> and <u>Good Guns Again</u> by Steve Bodio: Along the lines of <u>Best Guns</u> but more opinionated and quirky.

<u>Hell, I Was There</u> by Elmer Keith: The autobiography of a man who lived out West when the country was still relatively unspoiled and wild.

<u>A Sportsman's Notebook</u> by Ivan Turgenev: A "literary" book about hunting by the famous Russian author.

<u>Just Before Dark</u> by Jim Harrison: Fine essays about everything from food and wine (of course), to sports, to travel by one of the

country's best writers and truly one of its most rugged outdoorsmen. This guy goes into country I can only dream about.

Meditations on Hunting by Jose Ortega y Gasset. This classic work on the philosophy of hunting belongs in every sportsman's library.

A Taste of the Wild: A Compendium of Modern Game Cookery by A.J. McClane: One of the best, most thorough, and original on the subject we all hold dear to our stomachs.

Jake - A Labrador Puppy at Work and Play, and Upland Passage - A Field Dog's Education, both by Robert F. Jones: The first is for children, the second for adults or vice versa. Well written, and superbly illustrated by Bill Eppridge's photographs.

Ruffed Grouse published by Stackpole Books: A compendium of more than all but a few of us will ever want or need to know about this species.

The Ice-Shirt by William T. Vollman: The first volume of his in-progress Seven Dreams series. Rough, brutal, surreal stuff by one hell of a writer who is not yet thirty.

A Field Guide: Dog First Aid by Randy Acker, D.V.M. with Jim Fergus: The ultimate field guide for anyone who takes his dogs into the field. This book could help save your dog's life.

Bill Tarrant's Gun Dog Book— A Treasury of Happy Tails by Bill Tarrant: Great essays on bird dogs.

Dumb-bell of Brookfield, Pocono Shot and Other Great Dog Stories by John Taintor Foote: Seven of the greatest dog stories ever written.

Reel Deep In Montana's Rivers, Chasing Fish Tales, Waist Deep In Montana's Lakes, and Knee Deep In Montana's Rivers — all by John Holt: So what if I wrote them? They're good books, and if you come to Montana without a fly rod, you're making a mistake, and there's bird hunting in them. And I really need the money....

Kicking Up Trouble

was

edited by Steve Smith

and

designed by Ganay Johnson.